SEED OF ADAM
AND OTHER PLAYS

SEED OF ADAM

AND OTHER PLAYS

by

CHARLES WILLIAMS

With an Introduction by
ANNE RIDLER

GEOFFREY CUMBERLEGE
OXFORD UNIVERSITY PRESS
London   New York   Toronto

Oxford University Press, Amen House, London E.C. 4

GLASGOW NEW YORK TORONTO MELBOURNE WELLINGTON
BOMBAY CALCUTTA MADRAS KARACHI CAPE TOWN IBADAN

Geoffrey Cumberlege, Publisher to the University

First published   1948
Second impression 1954

REPRINTED LITHOGRAPHICALLY IN GREAT BRITAIN

B. and T.
11-1326 jay
11-30-59 cdm

INTRODUCTION

THE four plays here printed were written at intervals between 1936 and 1941, and at the time of his death in May 1945 Charles Williams was planning to collect them into a volume. Only one has yet appeared in print (*Seed of Adam*, a version of which was published in the periodical *Christendom*), but three have been produced on the stage; all were written because a producer wanted them, and all are practical plays.

Charles Williams had written for the stage many years before the earliest of these was begun. His first published play, *The Myth of Shakespeare*, appeared in 1928, and before this he had written several others for private occasions. *Three Plays* followed in 1931. But it was not until 1936 that his first really successful work of this kind appeared: in that year were produced *Cranmer of Canterbury*, commissioned by the Friends of Canterbury Cathedral for their summer festival, and *Seed of Adam*. For although most of the earlier works were commissioned, and so written with a performance in mind, they cannot be called plays in the sense that his later dramatic work can: they are better suited for reading than for acting—a kind of drama to which so many distinguished poets have contributed. Actually, the most interesting of the *Three Plays* (*The Chaste Wanton*) was the one not planned for production, and between these plays and the later group there was a startling development. What produced such a change in those five years, a change towards a truly personal idiom, which was not confined to his dramatic writing, but included his poetry too? I am inclined to think that the most important element in it was a change of metre. The point of view did not change—the effortless originality which marks any poem of Charles Williams's as his, however Pre-Raphaelite its diction—but as long as he was writing in blank verse, after the model of Lascelles Abercrombie (whose work he much admired at the time), he was liable to write in pseudo-Shakespearian metaphors, as in this passage (from *The Witch*):

> her words
> make of his ear a tiring-room to come
> thence like play-acting queens into his brain;

while the *Myth of Shakespeare* is a piece of deliberate and brilliant pastiche. But in those years of 1931–5 he was experimenting with a new metre for his series of poems about the Arthurian myths (the earlier versions were written in Pre-Raphaelite style); in those years, too, T. S. Eliot's first plays were published. The result was the much looser rhythm and the interior rhymes of *Cranmer* and *Seed of Adam*.

> Dullards of darkness, light's lazybones,
> poor primitives of our natural bareness,
> where's your awareness? will moans and groans
> for gold of brawn or brain regain
> the way to the entry of Paradise?

It is true that his language never became a colloquial language: he used a poetic diction to the last, but it became unmistakably his, and in these plays it does give the necessary illusion of colloquial speech.

> 'Surely that is Gabriel, that old gossip of heaven?'

> 'The house is full of things, and none right.'

There is, however, a change of approach as well as a change of speech: briefly, the use of symbolic instead of naturalistic characters to express his ideas. The figure of Satan in *The Rite of the Passion* perhaps foreshadows these later figures, and there are hints in the two Masques written for production at Amen House, but practically speaking, they were innovations in his work, and his use of them is, I think, his special contribution to the effort to recover a dramatic tradition. The Skeleton in *Cranmer* was originally conceived as two figures; he is commentator and actor at once, detached from the action, yet influencing it—a difficult poise which was, perhaps, even more successfully kept in the Flame of the final play (*The House of the Octopus*), which is used as a symbol of the Holy Spirit working in the world. In *Seed of Adam* there is no commentator (for the Chorus here does not comment), but the play is rich in dramatic symbols. Most interesting of them all is the fusion of Adam (Natural Man) with Caesar Augustus: when he orders the soldiers to make a census, there is a remarkable effect of compression—the audience feels the whole sweep of time from the creation of man down to the civilized organization of the Roman Empire, concentrated in this one moment before the Incarnation, and preparing for it. This play shows to perfection the myth-making power of Charles Williams's mind, for he has succeeded in making his characters both archetypal and particular. The same is true of *The House by the Stable* (the most widely performed of his plays) and its sequel *Grab and Grace*: the character of Man seems both universally true and personally lovable, and the Archangel Gabriel is both a celestial and a comic figure. And what could be more effective—or surprising—than the personification of Grace as an impish boy?

You could not say that Charles Williams consciously acquired dramatic technique, for he was preoccupied with ideas rather than with form; but drama was natural to him because ideas existed in a state of tension in his mind. Surely the dialectical method is a dramatic method, and if ever anyone's mind worked dialectically, it was his: as no one was better able to assess the value, the essential point, of a contrary opinion, so his own opinions often seemed to be reached through the clash of opposites, and to have in them the elements of both.[1] Thus, in his plays, the stuff of the drama

---

[1] Two passages from *The Religious Prospect* by V. A. Demant are relevant here: 'Two opposing positions are due to the break up of an original unity. So there is a common element in each pair of opposites. . . . (From them) something new emerges . . . which . . . stands in relation to the original unity as in some ways the same and in others not the same' (p. 139). 'Dogmatic religion . . . posits a dimension of reality running across the temporal order. In its sight the oppositions thrown up in the temporal order are not simple alternatives' (p. 146). It is this viewpoint which we reach in Charles Williams's plays.

is always the same: a conflict between good and evil which, almost always, resolves itself into a state where the old terms are no longer true, and what was originally seen as evil is also part of perfection. This is seen very clearly in *Seed of Adam*, where the Negress (Hell) becomes midwife at the Incarnation; but it happens in some sort in other plays too: in *The House by the Stable*, where Man's very foolishness is a source of joy—

> 'a mortal hand does more than the Domination';

in *The Death of Good Fortune* where 'all luck is good' (*all* luck); and elsewhere.[1] Hell is generally highly intelligent, and, up to a point, lucid about Heaven: witness the Third King in *Seed of Adam*. (The poignancy of the lines

> 'and angels by the way delayed us
> With exhortations of earnest heavenly evangels'

is due to their being spoken by him.) In *Grab and Grace* the devil is a comic figure and a subject for knockabout farce in the best tradition of the miracle plays. But even if Evil in this author's scheme may be, in the last resort, laughable because of its absurd pretensions, I do not think we ever feel that it is a dummy, put up to be knocked down, or that it is ever less than terrifying.

It is difficult to judge Charles Williams by contemporary standards other than those of his own work, and this is one result of his originality. He is eccentric to contemporary writing, but great enough to sustain and justify that lonely position; a dangerous model, but an admirable stimulant. By his own standards I rate *Seed of Adam* high, and two of the other plays are among the most pleasant of his writings: *The Death of Good Fortune* is the least interesting of the four, but it belongs with the rest. It is difficult, also, to give much idea of his poetry by quotation: it needs the context, from the pure fun of *Grab and Grace*, to the splendid

---

[1] In *The House of the Octopus* the apostasy of one girl saves the other Christians; in *Judgement at Chelmsford* the Accuser is really the Saviour, while Satan in the earlier *Rite of the Passion* played a similar part; and in *Cranmer* the denial is finally a source of greater strength.

rhetoric of *Seed of Adam*, and the lovely and tender closing scene of *The House by the Stable*. Fortunately the texts are here to speak for themselves.

These four plays should be considered together with *Cranmer of Canterbury* (Oxford University Press, 1936) and *The House of the Octopus* (Edinburgh House Press, 1945). Besides these, the best of his dramatic work, there is a pageant play, *Judgement at Chelmsford* (O.U.P., 1939), and two other plays written since the beginning of the war: *Terror of Light*, in prose, and *The Three Temptations*, a radio play. He was dissatisfied with *Terror of Light*, and intended some day to rewrite it in verse; *The Three Temptations* has not been included here, primarily because the book as it stands is the one which the author himself intended, and I was reluctant to depart from his intention; also because the play differs in technique from these four, having been designed for radio, and its place will be in a Collected Edition of the plays, if that comes to be published.

Seed of Adam was written at the request of Phyllis M. Potter, of the Chelmsford Diocesan Religious Drama Guild, for performance in that diocese. It was subsequently expanded, and has had twelve performances, three of them produced by Ruth Spalding, and the rest by Phyllis Potter. The other three plays were written for Ruth Spalding's company at Oxford. On the outbreak of war, Charles Williams moved there with the Oxford University Press, and she was then beginning to form the company which first worked in association with E. Martin Browne as the Oxford branch of the Pilgrim Players, and is now a separate organization under the name of the Rock Theatre Company. *The House by the Stable* and *The Death of Good Fortune* were written and produced in the autumn of 1939—the manuscripts are dated 26 October and 10 November respectively. Later, the same company gave performances of *The House by the Stable* in halls, air-raid shelters, garages, churches, schools, and theatres in many parts of the country; *The Death of Good Fortune* was also performed a good many times, in an expanded version. The former play was given by E. Martin Browne in a tour of north-western Europe in May 1945, and it has been broadcast (December 1945). *Grab and Grace* was composed between 5 and 14 August 1941, but various mischances prevented Ruth Spalding from producing it on the tour for which it was written, and so far it has not been put on the stage.

The text of each play is that of the latest version, with a few trifling corrections, where there were literal errors, or where exits and entrances had not been marked. As the author had, alas, not begun to prepare the book for press, the task of collating the scattered scripts has been a heavy one: this has been the sole responsibility of Raymond Hunt, who as Charles Williams's literary executor, and for many years before, has brought devotion and unsparing energy to the work of preserving and setting in order his writings. The text of *Seed of Adam* presented problems of its own, which are described in a note at the beginning of the play: as an Appendix, I have included the author's own synopsis, and some notes which he made for an address given after one of the performances. Although these last are incomplete, I have printed them because they give an idea of the working of his mind as he wrote.

Acknowledgements are due to Phyllis M. Potter (to whom the author had intended the dedication of *Seed of Adam*) and to Ruth Spalding for the loan of manuscripts and other material; also to Maurice Jacobson of the Curwen Press for advice on the Hebrew passage in *Seed of Adam*, and for providing a footnote on its pronunciation.

A. R.

June 1946

CONTENTS

xi

SEED OF ADAM

A NATIVITY PLAY

CHARACTERS

THE TSAR OF CAUCASIA (*King of Gold*)

HIS CHORUS

THE SULTAN OF BAGDAD (*King of Frankincense*)

HIS CHORUS

ADAM

EVE

JOSEPH

MARY

THE ARCHANGEL

TWO ROMAN SOLDIERS

THE THIRD KING (*King of Myrrh*), a Negro

MOTHER MYRRH (*Hell*), a Negress

The scene is before the house of Adam; to the right of it are the stables; on the left, at the front, the stump of a tree or a high stone

NOTE

THE only existing manuscript is that of the first version, printed in *Christendom*, September 1937. Of the second version, slightly expanded from the first, there are many typescripts which vary in accuracy, but after some difficulty I have identified the one which contains the author's own faint corrections. This is reproduced here, except that (*a*) the literal corrections necessary to all the scripts have been made; (*b*) two stage directions, added by the producer but approved by the author in performance, have been included on p. 9; and (*c*) the capitalization has been altered in one or two places to conform with the style of the other plays. The list of characters is compiled from the programmes used at the Brentwood and Oxford performances (1937 and 1939), both of which were approved by the author. It seemed best to combine the two, since I was uncertain which would have had his final approval. I should add, that in performance one alteration was required by the Censor.

RAYMOND HUNT

SEED OF ADAM

The TSAR *enters with some of the* CHORUS

CERTAIN VOICES. Juggle, sir; throw up the golden slivers.

OTHER VOICES. Sir, no; show rather the rivers,
   molten and golden streams; fertilizing, barricading,
   cities and nations, from stations of earth-edging Esquimaux
   to the hanging gardens of tropical sense:
   and there the high ships sailing, the deep ships unlading.

FIRST VOICES. Necklaces, bracelets, ear-rings; gaudies and gew-
   gaws!

OTHER VOICES. Purse rather and pocket of outer commerce; mind
   finding after kind, and all traffic its own.

THE TSAR. I am Gaspar,[1] Tsar of Caucasia;
   I sprang from our father Adam's loins
   in a bright emission of coins; Eve's need
   of gilded adornment nourished me to dig and dive.
   Pearls I brought up; springs I let forth: who
   will be beautiful now? who profitable then?
   Men thrive and I take my fee.
   Tricked out in riches half the world follow me;
   who fall, crawl or are kicked into dry ditches.

                    [*The* SULTAN *enters, with the rest of the* CHORUS

CERTAIN VOICES. Sir, play; throw up the notes of gold,
   or stir into silver smoke the rich incense.

OTHER VOICES. Sir, no; our old throats are tired.
   Show rather the philosophical plan,
   chess-playing, brick-laying, sooth-saying;
   the design of line, point, and curve.

FIRST VOICES. Titillate the brain by ear and eye!

OTHER VOICES. Build the austere academies to show why.

[1] Traditionally, Melchior is the King whose gift is gold. C. W. has
reversed Melchior and Gaspar, here and in an early poem. [*Ed.*]

3

THE SULTAN. I am Melchior, Sultan of Bagdad.
  Adam my father and Eve my mother
  construed me aloof from sister and brother
  through a post-paradisal afternoon.
  I build my mosques under a philosophical moon;
  I ride on the body's curves through spirals of air
  to the bare and rare domes of Bagdad my see.
  I give to whoever serves with me
  gnomic patterns of diagrammatic thrills.
  Half the world live in my train;
  who refrain, bereft of brain, are left to common ills.
SEMI-CHORUS. Give us the golden matter,
SEMI-CHORUS.   and the golden chatter,
THE CHORUS. for to-morrow everything begins again.
            [*They gather about the* KINGS, *some sitting or lying*
ADAM [*coming out of the house*]. Dullards of darkness, light's lazy-
    bones,
  poor primitives of our natural bareness,
  where's your awareness? will moans and groans
  for gold of brawn or brain regain
  the way to the entry of Paradise? up!
  shut your eyes, will you? or make a play
  for your leisure, and a treasure of your idleness? You,
  have you nothing better to do
  in our world but play hide and seek with oblivion?
  Say, say something, say
  who are you? I will tell you, tell you what you knew,
  I am Adam.
SEMI-CHORUS. Father Adam, the pasture is thin,
  the sheep and the hogs are thin, our coats
  button thinly about our throats
  thrawn with wind and thirsty for wine.
  Exchanges—his and mine—help us
  to bear with the bitterness of having nothing.

What should *we* do, feeling for Paradise?
Better to suck at the heel of the Tsar.

SEMI-CHORUS. Father Adam, if we go looking and snooping round
    corners,
we see terrible shapes trooping,
things eagle-beaked, giants with scimitars.
In Eden you found them friendly; here
what should we do but hide while they stride and deride
the bitterness of our having nothing?
Have you seen us slinking from those neighbourly taunts?
Better to go drinking the rhythms of the Sultan.

ADAM. If you found Paradise, you would find everything.

THE CHORUS. Call with the old bluster to muster by masses,
    and seek!

SOLO.   Speak civilly, father!
                        Where
shall we go? climb invisible cords into the air?
for road, river, and lane
are searched; it is not to be found.

THE CHORUS. And to-morrow everything begins again!

SOLO. What is this way? behind what sight or sound?

SOLO. He lost it, and he cannot say.

SOLO. There is not any.

SOLO.   Yes; it is bought for a penny
and slept off.

SOLO.   No; wise men have recognized
it is only our mothers' forms rationalized.

SOLO. The Tsar declares it is hope learning to grope.

SOLO. The Sultan says it is sensation living in negation.

SOLO. It is the loss of the one thing prized
masochistically advertized;

SOLO. or adolescence flushed with immature sense.

ADAM. Babies!

THE CHORUS. Who lost it?

5

ADAM.   I. What do you know,
  children, of what living on this earth is like then?

THE SULTAN. Father, you must not think you are everyone.

THE TSAR. Your children are men and women, and not you.

THE SULTAN. Individualized essence of you, perhaps;

THE TSAR. with each his particular Paradise in a nutshell.

THE SULTAN [*touching his lyre*]. Nuts! nuts!

THE TSAR [*throwing gold pieces*]. Nuts! nuts!

BOTH.   Nuts for the men-monkeys!
  Monkey-nuts! follow, follow, monkey-nuts!
  scratch and snatch for a portion of monkey-nuts!
  grab and grizzle for a ration of monkey-nuts!
  houp-la!

> [*The* CHORUS, *chattering and fighting, run about like
> monkeys. They gradually become involved in a general
> fierce battle and drift off, following the* KINGS, *with high
> shrieks*]

ADAM. I must set my law upon them; one thing first.

> [*He turns, meeting* EVE, *who has come out of the house at
> the noise*]

EVE. Are they fighting again?

ADAM.   What else?
  They have not the pain that in us stops us fighting.

EVE. Have they found anything?

ADAM.   Nothing, my Eve.
  They cannot find the centre, the core of the fruit
  where the root of return is. I dropped it; it is gone.
  Where is Mary?

EVE.   Mary has gone to the fair.

ADAM. Under the Mercy! . . . what is she doing there?

EVE. Watching mountebanks, laughing at clowns,
  applauding jugglers and tightrope walkers,
  listening to talkers, admiring lovers,

riding with children on the roundabout,
everywhere in the middle of the rout,
being, by her nature, all things to all men.

ADAM. Will she never discover any preference? any partial
liking for this where or that when?
Will she never care to marshal phenomena?
Cows, clowns, and crowns are alike to her—
has she not a trick of nursing the sick,
and as agile through all as the honey-plucking bee,
catching as much sweet there as from booths at the fair?
She must follow now another mind than mine.
I am set. Call Joseph; they shall be married.

EVE. Married! Mary? but why? and why Joseph?

ADAM. Lest I should die. She shall be wedded
lest our youngest born should be a prey
in her simplicity to her sisters and brothers.
I will not have her a scullion and a scorn
in the huts of Caucasia or the harems of Bagdad.
Joseph is a warlike and dutiful lad.
Call him.

EVE.   What is he, where is he, now?

ADAM. Lieutenant-general of the Sultan's horse,
an Islamite, a genius in cavalry tactics!
To see swung whole squadrons in the charge,
and—in a wild clatter of words breaking—flung
down the speaking of a poem, when the matter is sprung
to the flashing and slashing of a steel line
at the throat's blood. Hafiz taught him
and Omar; he outgenerals them; call him.

EVE. Will Mary have him?

ADAM.   As soon as any.
O pest on her for a zany of goodwill!

EVE. Husband!

ADAM.   Be easy. I am petulant. My want

7

worries at my throat, while she wants nothing,
nor ever sighs for nor even denies Paradise.
EVE. Paradise perhaps is hers and here.
ADAM. Among the sick or at the fair?—
Look, there she comes: call Joseph, I say.
He is in Bagdad's train. I must go again
to quieten their brawls. I will give them peace.
I will show them if I am Adam for nothing.

[JOSEPH *and* MARY *enter*

ADAM. Joseph, am I your lord?
JOSEPH.   In all things, sir,
under the justice of God.

ADAM.   Your father, Mary?
MARY. Sir, by the Direction.
ADAM.   It is well; hear me.
I do and undo; I am Adam. Paradise
shuts its last mouth upon us, and I am afraid.
It may be, after I have conquered yonder apes,
and shaped them to placabilities, that I shall find
by counting them some form unguessed,
some archangel disguised, some person or place
where is the grace of the Return. If, well;
if not, the thing this world must soon become
catches us up. Whether this be or not
I am determined you two shall be married.
A heart of purity and a mind of justice
to be integrity. What say you?
JOSEPH.   Sir,
I am of no more worth to the princess Mary
than the fly-flick of her mule's tail.
MARY.   But as much, Joseph, indeed.
JOSEPH. You hear, my lord?
ADAM.   Never mind her.
Since she loves all, she loves you. What of you?

JOSEPH. She is the manifest measurement of God's glory
correcting time.

ADAM [*motioning them before him*]. You are both my best of
children.

[JOSEPH *and* MARY *kneel ;* ADAM *raises his right arm*
By the single indecipherable Name
I swear you, Joseph and Mary, to betrothal.

[JOSEPH *and* MARY *rise and face each other. The upraised
palms of their right hands touch. They turn to face* ADAM]
When I return from conquering the world, be ready,
as then shall be, in time and space, convenient.
Come, Eve.

[ADAM *and* EVE *go out*

JOSEPH. Am I appointed for your husband? . . .
Answer, princess . . . no ? no then, do not speak,
do not break through such an outgoing stress of light,
as is the sovereign blessedness of the world,
there indivisible, all ways else divisible.
Do not with descent, O altitude, even of mercy,
sweeten the enhancèd glance of those still eyes
which to my lord's house, and to me the least,
illumine earth with heaven, our only mortal
imagination of eternity,
and the glory of the protonotary Gabriel.

[MARY *stretches out her hand to him ; he kneels and kisses it*
MARY [*murmuring the name*]. Gabriel, Gabriel : well spoken is the
name.
As I came from the fair I looked back ; there
I saw it all in a sheath and a shape of flame,
having an eagle's head that turned each way
as if it were guarding something and looking for something.
Its eyes burned at me ; the noise
of the hurly-burlies and the hurdy-gurdies,
the ball-spinners, the silk-sellers, the rum-peddlers,

9

the swings, and the songs, rose to a whirring voice,
the air was a hum of sound; I heard it come
as if the fair all rose in the air and flew
on eagle's wings after me; I ran
through the fear and the laughter and the great joys.
I came by the vineyards to my father's roof;
there it held aloof a little.
I saw you; I gave you my hand, Joseph,
at my father's will. It has still power,
this hand of Adam's daughter, on all creatures of heaven.

JOSEPH [*as he kneels*].   O princess,
your hand is the fact of God's compact of light.

MARY. I have heard such talk among the lovers at the fair.
Bless you for telling me, Joseph.

> [*He releases her hand. The* ARCHANGEL *appears at the
> back, as it were casting sleep towards* JOSEPH, *who sinks
> slowly forward, and lies still*]

MARY.   Joseph!

[*A pause*

Joseph!

[*She sees him lying*

THE ANGELIC CHORUS [*without*]. Adonai Elohim! Adonai Elohim![1]
THE ARCHANGEL [*standing behind* MARY]. Adonai hu ha-elohim!
THE CHORUS [*as the angelic army without*]. Shalom lach eschet-chen,
    Adonai immach beruchah at bannashim.

  Al-tiri Miryam ki-matsat chen lifne ha-elohim.

  Vehinnach harah veyoladt ben vekaret et-shemo Yeshua.

MARY. How shall these things be, seeing I know not a man?
THE CHORUS. Ruach hakkodesh tavo alayieh ugevurat elyon tatsel
    alayich: al ken Kadosh yeamer layyillod ben-ha-elohim.

---

[1] The Hebrew is written phonetically, as for the Sephardi pronunciation
(vowel sounds as in Italian, all *r*'s distinctly sounded, *ch* as in *loch*). The
Ashkenazi pronunciation can be used if desired.

MARY. Behold the handmaid of the Lord; be it unto me
according to thy word.

> [*The* ARCHANGEL *passes round and enters the stables.* MARY
> *remains rapt*]

JOSEPH [*he rises to his knees, as before, and wakes*]. Under the
Protection! Mary . . . Mary . . .

MARY. Yes, Joseph?

JOSEPH. Mary, you are changed; you are in love.

MARY. Yes, Joseph.

JOSEPH [*starting up*]. Ah, ah! but who . . . ?

MARY. No one, Joseph.
Only in love.

JOSEPH. It must be then with someone.

MARY. Dearest, you did not hear: we said *in love*.
Why must, how can, one be in love with someone?

JOSEPH. Because . . . but that is what *in love* means;
one is, and can only be, in love with someone.

MARY. Dearest, to be in love is to be in love,
no more, no less. Love is only itself,
everywhere, at all times, and to all objects.
My soul has magnified that lord; my spirit
rejoiced in God my saviour; he has regarded
the nothingness of his handmaid. He has thrust
into this matter his pattern of bones, as Eve's
towers of cheeks and arrogant torches of eyes
edify red earth into a pattern of manhood.

JOSEPH. But it must be at some time and in some place.

MARY. When you look at me, dear Joseph, do you think so?

JOSEPH. Babylonia and Britain are only boroughs of you.
Your look dimensions the world. I took once
a northward journey to find fables for the Sultan
and heard a lad on the hill of Faesulae syllabling
a girl of Faesulae who nodded good-morning at him,
and that her form timed the untimed light.

Place must be because grace must be,
and you because of glory. O blessing,
the light in you is more than you in the light.

MARY. The glory is eternal, and not I,
and I am only one diagram of the glory:
will you believe in me or in the glory?

JOSEPH. It is the vision of the Mercy.

MARY.   Hold to that.
But for salvation—even of those who believe
that time and place and the one are the whole of love—
Love—O the Mercy! the Protection!—
shall make his flesh as one in time and place.
It shall come in the time of Augustus Caesar,
in the place of Bethlehem of the Holy Ghost,
in the coast of Judaea: not quite Jerusalem,
but not far from Jerusalem, not far but not quite.
O Thou Mercy, is this the secret of Thy might?
When Thou showest Thyself, that Thou art not there
to be found? we find Thee where Thou art not shown.
Thou art flown all ways from Thyself to Thyself,
and Thy ways are our days, and the moment is Thou.
O Thou Mercy, is this the thing to know?
Joseph, come, take me to Bethlehem;
there the apparition and the presence are one,
and Adam's children are one in them;
there is the way of Paradise begun.

> [*They move round the stage to the stone. As they go, the*
> CHORUS *re-enter on all sides*]

THE CHORUS. In Thule, in Britain, in Gaul, in Rome,
among the slim pillars of Bagdad, in round mounds of Caucasia,
we heard the maxim that rules the schools of prophets:
this also is Thou; neither is this Thou.

With double hands and single tongues
the prophets climb the rungs of heaven,

in the might of a maxim gained and given:
this also is Thou; neither is this Thou.

But we who wander outside the rules and schools
compromise and complain,
before the clot in the blood has shot to the heart or brain:
this is not quite Thou and not quite not.

Sister, sister, did you dream?

What did you see on the banks of the body's stream,
in Thule, in Britain, in Gaul, in Rome,
under Bagdad's dome, by the mounds of Caucasia?
SOLO. One came walking over the sand,
one and a shadow from a desert land;
I saw a knife flash in a black hand.

At daybreak a child is born to the woman;
he grows through the noon to his full stature;
she devours him under the moon; then at morn—
THE CHORUS. Save us, Father Adam, or we perish!—
SOLO. or in a mirage of morn the child is reborn.
And to-morrow everything begins again.
THE CHORUS. From bone, from brain, from breasts, from hands,
from the mind's pillars and the body's mounds,
the skies rise and roll in black shadows
inward over the imperial soul:
over our sighs in the moon of dusty sorrow—
O, O, could everything begin before to-morrow;
over the creak of rusty grief—
to-morrow will be soon enough for belief;
over the kitchens of a pot neither cold nor hot,
and the thin broth, and the forming of the clot—
not quite Thou and not quite not.

Father Adam, save us or we perish.

[MARY *sits on the stone,* JOSEPH *stands behind her. From*

13

opposite sides two ROMAN SOLDIERS *run in, turn to the
front, and come to the salute*]

FIRST SOLDIER. Octavianus Caesar Augustus,
SECOND SOLDIER. filius Julii divi Augustus,
BOTH SOLDIERS. orders the world in the orbit of Rome.
FIRST SOLDIER. Oaths and service to the lord Augustus;
SECOND SOLDIER. incense and glory to the god Augustus:
BOTH SOLDIERS. to the god Augustus and the Fortune of Rome.

> [*They wheel inwards, and fall back on either side.* ADAM
> *re-enters as* AUGUSTUS, *accompanied by* EVE *and the two*
> KINGS]

ADAM. I was Julius, and I am Octavianus,
Augustus, Adam, the first citizen,
the power in the world, from brow to anus,
in commerce of the bones and bowels of men;
sinews' pull, blood's circulation,
Britain to Bagdad. I in brawn and brain
set knot by knot and station by station.
I drive on the morrow all things to begin again.
Look, children, I bring you peace;
I bring you good luck; I am the State; I am Caesar.
Now your wars cease; what will you say?

THE TSAR. Hail, Caesar; I am your occupation for the days.
THE SULTAN. I am your sleeping-draught for the nights: hail,
Caesar.
THE CHORUS. Hail, Caesar; we who are about to die salute you!
ADAM. I will take now a census of the whole world,
the nations and generations of the living and dead,
to find whether anywhere it has been said
what place or person Paradise lies behind,
even among the prophets who made a formula for the mind.
Each man shall answer, on or under earth,
from Cain and Abel, who were first to explore
womb and tomb, and all whom women bore,

14

to the pack that died at Alexandria yesterday.
Answer, children, and say, if you can. I know
the thing that was threatened comes; there is still time.
Go!

> [*The* SOLDIERS *run out; there is a deep and confused noise.*[1]
> *Presently they return, bearing papers*]

FIRST SOLDIER. All these millions dead

SECOND SOLDIER.   and dying; these thousands
   dying or dead;

FIRST SOLDIER.   these hundreds, and sixteen—

> [*He drops his spear towards the nearest of the* CHORUS *on
> his side, who answers as from a sepulchre*]

ONE OF THE CHORUS. and seventeen

ANOTHER.   and eighteen

ANOTHER.   and nineteen

> [*All answer in turn, as the* FIRST SOLDIER, *and then the*
> SECOND, *pass, pointing their spears. The* SECOND *comes to*
> JOSEPH]

JOSEPH [*answering according to the number of the* CHORUS]. and
   thirty-six

> [*The* SOLDIER *points to* MARY

JOSEPH [*answering for her*]. and thirty-seven.
   Shall I add one more for the child that slumbers in your womb?

---

[1] The producer suggested that something should be added here, and
used to prepare for the entrance of the Third King shortly afterwards.
C. W. had begun to write this additional matter, but the following
fragment is all that we have:

   TSAR. When the Archangel spoke to you in the true Paradise
      and your heart broke—what did he say, there
      under the trees? something you could not hear
      about not-dying
   SULTAN.   When you ran and pushed
      your way through hedge and river, when you rushed
      down the ledge of rock between the abounding foliage
      near the water rounding Paradise and the world outside—
      a few leaves of the hedge clung to your coats
   TSAR. a few drops of water hung on your skins.
      That was the beginning.
   SULTAN.   Twinning what was one

MARY. O no, Joseph; he is something different from all numbers;
   you cannot tell how or whom. The people are reckoned,
   but the child that comes through me
   holds infinity in him, and hides in a split second.

> [*The* SOLDIERS *return to* ADAM

FIRST SOLDIER. Hail, Caesar; those who are dead

SECOND SOLDIER.   and those about to die

BOTH SOLDIERS. salute you.
   Octavianus Caesar Augustus;
   filius Julii divi Augustus;
   gubernator, imperator, salvator, Augustus.

A VOICE [*off*]. What is this difference between the dying and the
   dead?

> [*The* THIRD KING *enters, followed by a* NEGRESS, *carrying*
> *a scimitar*]

ALL [*except* JOSEPH *and* MARY, *in a general moan*]. Ah!

THIRD KING [*looking round*]. What provincial talk is this? what
   academic
   pedantic dichotomy? O la, brothers!

> [*Seeing the* KINGS *left, right*

THE TWO KINGS. Ah, brother, how did you find us?

THIRD KING. Indeed I might not have done;
   but my mother here has eyes and a nose,
   and with each sun recognized more strongly
   gold's glint and censer's smell.
   As the wind of infinity blows
   earth is always leaving clues for hell,
   and hell has only to follow that news of earth.
ᵀ*To the* CHORUS]
   No wonder you talk so if you have them here
   talking of distinctions and differences, smells and savours,
   sight of gold, sniff of incense, flavours
   of this or that differing degree of corruption.

[*To the* KINGS]

    You left me away in a stony land,
    brothers; I was lonely without you.
    I came to find this mind of Rome,
    this concept, this Augustus, this new Adam.
    Why, father! The old Adam, after all!

ADAM. It is you, is it?

THIRD KING.   I. You saw me
    when you breathlessly slid down the smooth threshold
    of Paradise gate? and saw the things that were hid
    as God warned you you would? did you know
    I was the core of the fruit you ate?
    Did you remember, ungrateful that you are,
    how you threw me away, with such a swing
    I flew over Eden wall, dropped,
    and stuck between two stones?
    You did not see; you did not look after me!
    Smell and taste for you; let the core go to hell.
    But God looks after the sparrows.
    Presently the sun split the core,
    and out grew I, the King of the core.
    I have travelled to get back to you ever since.

EVE. And who is she?

THIRD KING.   Ah, she!
    At the heart of the core, in the core of me,
    lived a small worm you could not see.
    The sun is a generous sun; he set us both free.
    She lives by me, and I by her.
    I call her my little mother Myrrh,
    because of her immortal embalming. We two
    have come, my other mother, to live with you—
    if you can call it living.

ADAM.   What else?

THIRD KING. O well! She has her own idea of food.

> [*He indicates the scimitar*

The nearer the relation, the better the dish.
But you will not *die*; no, I do not think you will *die*.
I did not, and I have been eaten often,
you may imagine; it was a long way from here,
and a long time ago, that we made our start,
and angels on the way delayed us,
with exhortations of earnest heavenly evangels:
but what can angels do against decaying matter?
Matter can only be corrected by matter,
flesh by flesh; we came through and came on,
and I everlastingly perishing. The worm
of that fruit, father, has a great need to feed
on living form. But I do not think you will die.

ADAM [*to the* SOLDIERS]: Seize her.

> [*They rush forward. She laughs at them, and they fall back
> on their knees*]

THIRD KING.   Whom are you seeking?
Are you come out with swords and staves to take us?
We were often with you in your temples: now—
Father Adam, you were always a fool,
and it seems at the top of your Roman school
no better; will you arrest the itch
with your great hands? will your bands pitch
their javelins against the diabetes of the damned?
The belly is empty in hell though the mouth is crammed:
a monotonous place!

THE CHORUS.   Father Adam, lord Augustus!

THIRD KING. Among the stones and locusts she lived on me;
it is your turn—this is my refrigerium.

> [*He draws back. The* TWO KINGS *drop their gold and lute.*
> EVE *covers her face. The* NEGRESS *walks slowly round, the*

18

CHORUS *falling on their knees as she passes. At last she*
comes to MARY. *Meanwhile the* CHORUS]

THE CHORUS. Call the kings!

saints! poets!

prophets! priests!

Call the gospels and the households!

those of Aquino and Assisi!

Stratford! Chalfont St. Giles!

caskets of Caucasia!

censers of Bagdad!

ALL. Help us and save us!

THE TWO KINGS. Balthazar our brother is stronger than we.

THE CHORUS. Call on the households!

harp-stringer of David!

hewer of wood for Joseph!

ink-maker for Virgil!

galley-captain of Caesar!

armour-bearer of Taliessin!

ALL. Come to your defences! all heavenly lords,

stand about us with swords.

THIRD KING. Election is made, capital rather than coast:

she thrives most on the dear titbits of perfection.

Sister, you are lovelier than all the rest,

and like the busy blest. She shall eat you alive

for her great hunger; take pity on her appetite.

[JOSEPH, *drawing his own scimitar, thrusts himself between*
them]

JOSEPH [*crying out*]. Ha, ha! to me, my household!

There is no God but God: in the name of God!

[*The scimitars clash; the* THIRD KING *touches* JOSEPH *in the*
thigh; he stumbles and is beaten down]

THIRD KING [*dragging him away*]. Little man, martyrs and con-
fessors

are no good here, nor are poets any good.

They are all a part of the same venomous blood.

Come away, come away, and wait your turn quietly.

> [MARY *takes a step or two forward*

MARY. Dearest, you will find me very indigestible.

The stomach of the everlasting worm

is not omnivorous; it is a poor weak thing:

nor does the fire of Gehenna do more than redden

the pure asbestos of the holy children; if mine,

is for the fire and your dangerous appetite to find.

> [*The* NEGRESS *attacks* MARY *with her scimitar.* MARY *goes
> back before her, at first slowly, moving round the stage*]

MARY. Sister, how slowly you carve your meat!

THIRD KING. Be easy, sister; you will not get away from us.

MARY. Nor she from me, brother, which is more important.

> [*The movement of the two women quickens and becomes a
> dance; the scimitar flashing round them in a white fire.
> The* CHORUS *sway to the movement,* ADAM *only remaining
> motionless*]

MARY [*suddenly breaking into song*]. Parturition is upon me:
blessed be He!

Sing, brothers; sing, sisters; sing, Father Adam.

My soul magnifies the Lord.

THE CHORUS [*hesitatingly*]. My spirit hath rejoiced in God my
saviour.

MARY [*dancing and singing*]. For he hath regarded the low estate
of his handmaid:

THE CHORUS [*gathering strength*]. behold, from henceforth all
generations shall call thee blessed.

> [MARY *at the door of the stable, where the* ARCHANGEL *is
> seen, catches the uplifted wrist of the* NEGRESS *in her right
> hand. They stand rigid, foot to foot*]

MARY [*singing joyously through a profound suspense*]. For he that is
mighty hath done to me great things;

THE NEGRESS [*in a shriek of pain and joy*]. and holy is his Name.
[*She faints at* MARY'*s feet*

MARY [*leaning towards* JOSEPH]. Joseph!
My son calls to his foster-father: come!
prince of maidens, hasten to the master of maidenhoods,
and the pillar of maternity.

JOSEPH [*half-rising*]. O mother of the world's brightness,
I sought uprightness, and yet it failed in the end!

MARY. Most dear friend, my lord, it delayed the scimitar
but till my son took flesh under its flash:
the heavens constrain me to glory: Joseph!
[*He springs up and to her, and takes her into the stable*

ADAM [*in a strong voice*]. His mercy is on them that fear him from
generation to generation.
[*The* CHORUS, *singing, gather about the* TWO KINGS, *as at
first*]

FIRST CHORUS. He hath showed strength with his arm;

SECOND CHORUS. he hath scattered the proud in the imagination
of their hearts.

FIRST CHORUS. He hath put down the mighty from their seats;

SECOND CHORUS. and exalted them of low degree.

FIRST CHORUS. He hath filled the hungry with good things;

SECOND CHORUS. and the rich he hath sent empty away.

THIRD KING [*stretching out his hand towards the* CHORUS]. Are you
now so gay?
[*As his hand sinks down, they fall on their knees*
And you, lord Adam,
do not speak too soon; you desired the boon of salvation—
have it! You desired twice—me and not me,
the turn and the Return; the Return is here,
take care that you do not now prefer me.

JOSEPH [*coming from the stable*]. Sir, send a midwife to your
daughter.

All things are rigid; only Mary and I
move, and the glory lies even between us.
The Return is at point to issue; befriend salvation.

> [*All the figures are rigid, except* JOSEPH *and the* THIRD
> KING. ADAM *speaks with difficulty and without moving*]

ADAM. Whom shall I send? whom?

THIRD KING. We, call we you father, are not yours;
we are the things thought of before you, brought
into Eden while men were not, when
in the Days hunger was created, and lives
with a need always to feed on each other. This
was felt in the first kiss of man and woman.
Mother, there is a good cake for you now
to take everlastingly; go, kiss her, love
hungers: deliver her and she shall deliver you.

> [*The* NEGRESS *leaps up and turns on him*

The eaten are on your left hand, the uneaten on your right;
go—there is no thing living so dextrous as you.

> [*The* NEGRESS *and* JOSEPH *go into the stable*

THE ARCHANGEL. Adonai hu ha-elohim!

THIRD KING. What do you see, man? but I see.
Flesh is become that firmament of terrible crystal
your prophet saw: within it wreathed amber
and fire sheathed in the amber; now
the fire and the amber and the crystal are mingled into form;
what do you hear, man? [*He pauses*] but I hear
the terrible sound of the crystal singing as it spins
round the amber where the fire is hidden, and now the amber
is hidden in the crystal, and the crystal spinning into flesh,
twining into flesh: it slows, it stops, it sinks—
what do you know, man? but I know—
it drops into the stretched hands of my mother;
my mother has fetched a child from the womb of its mother;

22

my mother has taken the taste of the new bread.
Adonai Elohim!

[JOSEPH *comes from the stable*

JOSEPH. Father Adam, come in; here is your child,
here is the Son of Man, here is Paradise.
To-day everything begins again.

[ADAM *goes down to the door of the stable*

MARY [*meeting him and genuflecting*]. Bless me, father: see how
to-morrow is also now.

ADAM [*making the sign of the Cross*]. Under the Protection!
peace to you, and to all; goodwill to men.

[*They go into the stable*

JOSEPH. Our father Adam is gone in to adore.

THE TSAR. Blessed be he who is the earth's core

THE SULTAN. and splits it all ways with intelligible light.

THE CHORUS. Christ bring us all to the sight
of the pattern of glory which is only he.

THE ARCHANGEL. Yeshua!

THE TSAR. Blessed be he whose intelligence came to save
man from the gripping of the grave: blessed be he.

THE SULTAN. Blessed be he who, because he does all things well,
harries hell by his mercy: blessed be he.

THIRD KING. Blessed be he who is the only Necessity
and his necessity in himself alone.

EVE. Blessed be he who is sown in our flesh, grown
among us for our salvation: blessed be he.

THE CHORUS. Christ bring us, by his clean pact,
into the act which is only he.

THE ARCHANGEL. Yeshua!

THIRD KING. He consumes and is consumed.

THE SULTAN. He is the womb's prophecy and the tomb's.

THE TSAR. He creates, redeems, glorifies: blessed be he.

EVE. He is all our heart finds or lacks.

JOSEPH. He frees our souls from hell's cracks.

23

THE CHORUS. Christ bring us, by his true birth,
  into a new heaven and earth.

JOSEPH. Blessed be he whose love is the knowledge of good
  and its motion the willing of good: blessed be he.

THE CHORUS. Adore, adore: blessed for evermore
  be the Lord God Sabaoth: blessed be He.

THE DEATH OF
GOOD FORTUNE

A CHRISTMAS PLAY

CHARACTERS

MARY

GOOD FORTUNE

THE KING

THE LOVER

THE MAGICIAN

THE OLD WOMAN

THE YOUTH

THE GIRL

The scene is an open place in a city

THE DEATH OF GOOD FORTUNE

MARY. Incipit vita nova: substance is love,
  love substance. Begins substance to move
  through everywhere the sensuality of earth and air.
  I was its mother in its beginning: I taught
  the royal soothsayers to follow a moving star,
  and brought them to their primal, far, and hierarchical Head.
  I am Wisdom whose name is Mary. I wept by the Dead.
  I arose with the Arisen. I see now
  where terribly through all spheres of gods and men
  pulse his ambiguous life and death dealing vibrations.
  His are all the alterations: and here shall be ours.
  There is on earth a being called Good Luck;
  he has spun much joy; his nature is heavenly,
  but when men fell, he was half-blinded;
  he does not know himself nor do men know him.
  I have determined that in this town this very day
  this gay popular lord shall come to his change
  and a strange new vision of himself; for now
  my lord my Son has made this clear—
  that all luck is good luck. And I,
  I struck by seven swords, witness too
  that all substance is love, all luck is good.
  Nor anywhere, for any flood of shed blood,
  sharp single anguish, or long languish of grief,
  shall any deny my word, or the great cry
  to every man upon earth of my lord your Son—
  all chance is heavenly, all luck is good.
  Let us see Good Fortune come now to his trance.
    [*She seats herself. The* OLD WOMAN *enters with a* YOUTH
THE OLD WOMAN. This is where the king will come; stay here.
THE YOUTH. Everything is gay this morning; see how the fair

glows in the market: the tumblers calling and springing
and the jugglers flinging their quoits. I will go there
when we have seen the king. I will wrestle or cast
a hammer as fast and as far as their own champions.
I will be no puny challenger. Hey,
the blood runs quick this fair morning.
Will you speak to the king yourself, great aunt?

THE OLD WOMAN. Yes.

They say that since his new guest came
the king will do all he is asked. I will task him little.
He could give me a house without hurting himself,
and will, I hope: there is good luck in the air.

THE YOUTH. And then I will go to the fair; I would fain see
the humped long-necked beast they call a camel
or a man fight, as they say he does naked,
with the wild long-toothed tiger from Seringapatam.

THE OLD WOMAN. Whatever you like.

THE YOUTH. So I will. Who
is the king's new friend, to please him so?

THE OLD WOMAN. People like us do not know the lords' names,
only their acts. He came walking one day
into the city, under a bright sky,
himself as light and gay as that morning or this;
he was clearly a noble prince. Where he went
every event seemed better, every chance the happier.
That day I added to my store a piece of gold,
and all my neighbours told like good luck.

[*Enter the* LOVER *and the* MAGICIAN

THE LOVER. O but since he came, this king's friend,
this lord, this miracle-worker, even my fortune
seems to have grown greater. I love more,
and there is more joy in my more love.
There is a neat trick about the moments
that brings me to my sweet at any odd time

28

when my heart is like to break not to see her.

THE MAGICIAN. It may well be: he says his name is Good Fortune.

THE LOVER. I can believe it indeed: he is all aerial.

O Good Fortune, be my god, and bless
me with her, and both of us with you.

THE MAGICIAN. He is like the full profession of my best art
gone out of itself into mankind.
We find too often the last prophecies are lost
at their end in a mist of faint knowledge. He,
this god—call you him so—at least this star,
came to the city in a dazzle. That I foresaw:
the law of the planets foretold a great event—
which must be he: unless beyond the bound
of all sidereal traffic, there were something more—
but that no astrology has ever found.

THE OLD WOMAN. Sir, will the king come soon?

THE LOVER.   Soon.

THE MAGICIAN. Nay, it seems no one even waits now:
lo, the king, and—do we say a star?

THE LOVER. Star or daemon—call him our god Good Fortune.

> [*The* KING *enters with* GOOD FORTUNE, *the* MAGICIAN'*s
> daughter attending*]

THE KING. This city, that holds all our lives,
thrives well; but now you are come,
our lord Good Fortune, it has a spell within it
to be fortunate for ever; strangers shall see and say
how our devotion praises in the phases of its passage
only you; to you is all our homage.
Here we rule best and love best;
here knowledge finds wisdom and age rest.
Happy are you, Good Fortune, and we in you.
Deign only to maintain your grace in this place.

GOOD FORTUNE. I am Good Fortune, satisfaction, the action of the
heart

when all goes well. I have made this your city
my divine choice; mine while I care to stay—
and I think now I shall not leave you; I
have a power of fidelity too, and it may be true
that I shall stay here and enjoy you; your town
shall be known everywhere for a nest of young delight,
a camp of successful joys, and a rest for the old.
I am always young, a giver of good things,
and you here, by my mere arbitrary choice,
I deign to gratify; cry then my praise;
no god is stronger than I except Pan,
and Pan and I have divided the world between us.

MARY. It is known everywhere that Pan is already dying,
for the substance of love takes him with great shocks;
and you too, fair lord, shall find what locks
were broken for ever when my Son strode through hell.

THE KING. It is true; my armies, since you came, win
on all my frontiers; where my enemies entered in,
they are thrown back; victory is mine alone.
I have good chance now to reward good service.

THE OLD WOMAN. My husband's blood being shed then for you
in one of your fights, and he dead, great sir,
grant me the reward of his service; grant me a house
for old bones to lie securely. No alms;
only my own roof. I have saved; it lies
hidden in my lodging, but the lodging is dank and rank
with the smells of the butchers' quarter. I would rather live
in the new houses you, my king, have built
beyond the river: besides, now I live
with my son and his wife; we cannot get on together.
She is young and bitter and I am old and tired.
My husband died for you; give me now
a proper lodging where I can live on my savings.

THE KING. Willingly; take which you choose: our lord here

 smiles on all petitions, and I allow,
 I would do also anything for my friends here
 but they do not need it; their ends are beyond me:
 yours is in your maid and yours in your art.
 Yet my heart is apt to give: is there none?
 and you?

THE GIRL. Nothing.

THE MAGICIAN.   Nothing?

THE GIRL.   What else?
 Can you, father, or your new god Good Luck
 help me in a world where despair only is true?
 No; if that is a god, I am an atheist.
 I will wait a little to see if your god will die.

GOOD FORTUNE. Do you say, girl, that I am bound to die?

THE GIRL. I say I do not believe in you; nothing more.

GOOD FORTUNE. Look round; see them happy; will not you be?
 Worship me, and see what I can do.

THE GIRL. I have lived long enough on earth to know
 that earth has no new birth of good luck.

GOOD FORTUNE. But I am not of earth; I am aerial,
 born in the mid heavens, a prince of the zodiac,
 heir to fine fantasies, lacking nothing.
 Will you take them as a gift?

THE GIRL.   No; they exist nowhere.
 They are the twist of man's heart to defend itself.
 You may come from the middle air, but you are deceit
 if you do; your feet have no print on our soil.

MARY. He is deceit indeed, but only because
 he does not know how great a prince he is.
 Since my Son died, all things are good luck,
 and fate and good luck and heaven are one name.

GOOD FORTUNE. Am I defrauded in my chosen town?

ALL THE OTHER PERSONS.   No.
 Lord, she is obstinate, false, heretical;

    she will stick at nothing to make herself great:
    abate displeasure; treasure us instead.

THE KING. Cense we now, in divine ritual, this godhead.

THE LOVER. Tread we the circle; beat we the solemn vow.

THE YOUTH [*to the* OLD WOMAN]. Shall we go?

THE OLD WOMAN.   We cannot.

THE YOUTH.   Why? the fair waits.
    Must we stand by while the king ceremonializes?
    let's to the prizes! let's to the loud noise!

THE OLD WOMAN. Hist! you will do better if you worship the god.
                [*The ceremony of censing; during which—*

MARY. Before the advent of the necromantic kings
    in the beginning, I saw a star sliding,
    shining, guiding their god-divining caravan.
    Its name was called *TYXH*, its flame was fortune,
    its messenger and shape on earth was this lord here,
    whose sphere above attended my Son's birth;
    but he, being blinded by cloud, is half-minded
    to glorify himself for only half his worth;
    I must teach him all: it is time that he should die.

GOOD FORTUNE. Ah! . . . rocks the earth, or was it I?

THE KING. God, what frightened you?

GOOD FORTUNE.   What lightened then
    or did my eyes dazzle?

                [*He leans on the* LOVER

THE LOVER.   Your hand is cold !
    what is the matter, our God?

GOOD FORTUNE.   My head splits!

THE OLD WOMAN. You have cramp in the stomach, or else the damp airs
    of the valley have given you a chill.

GOOD FORTUNE.   My spirit is flung
    into fits of terror!

THE MAGICIAN. He is rigid in a seizure.

GOOD FORTUNE. Ah!

[*He falls*

THE KING. You—look! what ails him?

THE MAGICIAN. I did not dare
even to fear this—

THE GIRL. But I—I knew.

THE YOUTH. Come; you promised; let us get to the fair.
Our lords die; are we to cry their wake?
Take we a quiet—

THE OLD WOMAN. I am afraid! hush!
Be quiet yourself, you fool!

THE MAGICIAN. Must I look?
Must I think that this god can die?
Must I think that a secretly-sliding star
that the gods neglect has struck this lord of Good Luck?
When that hiding opens—

[*He kneels by him and stands up*

He is dead.

THE OLD WOMAN. Dead?

THE KING. He—*he* dead?

THE YOUTH. All the fair has stopped! what has happened?

THE LOVER. This god cannot die.

THE MAGICIAN. So? And yet he is dead.

[*They all stare at* GOOD FORTUNE; *then they look at each other*

And what will happen now?

THE GIRL. O woe!
I did not quite believe it!

THE LOVER. But if Good Fortune
is dead . . .

THE OLD WOMAN. The money! the money I hid away
to spend on my own living, and save my head
from having at last to lie in a bed lent

D   33

by my son's wife grudgingly till I died. . . .
Come!

THE YOUTH. But the fair?

THE OLD WOMAN. Curse the fair! Come.

[She hurries him out

THE LOVER. If Good Fortune is dead, what will happen to love?

THE MAGICIAN. What indeed?

THE KING. To the Kingdom?

THE MAGICIAN. What indeed?

THE LOVER. The city, he said, is a place of youth; if
Good Fortune . . . and how much is truth a part of Good
Fortune?

THE GIRL. Not at all: that I do know: not at all.

[He stares at her and rushes out

THE MAGICIAN. Sir, will you not also hurry to see
about the frontiers? are no fears growing in you?

THE KING. Yes.

[He begins to go, and returns
Do you try first: can you spy
by your tables of magic the truth of this? Try.

THE MAGICIAN. My art was my heart, as her savings and his love
and your royalty were hearts' realms too; it is sped
if this lord of fortunate chances is indeed dead.

THE GIRL. Father—

THE MAGICIAN. Hush! If your atheism was right,
plight yourself to it, but do not now speak.

THE KING. Try.

THE MAGICIAN. I will try—to please you, and to satisfy
myself that what I feared might come has come.

[He lifts his wand
I lift the hazel rod in the banishing pentagram
against the god of illusion, against Lilith the accurst:
depart, incubi and succubi! depart, phantoms;
I call on the stars of heaven in their even rule,

34

exact powers, to show me the fact happening.
Show me the measured fate of this kingdom: show!

[He speaks to the KING

Your enemies move on your borders; in the front line
your orders are frustrated; one of your towns is on fire;
your reserves are belated in the forest. This god
shall be waited on soon by many men,
and your kingdom be past and your crown given to another,
because the curse of the death of Good Luck is come, and . . .

[He tries to see

THE KING. Look; look forward but a month!
THE MAGICIAN. Good Luck is dead: I can see nothing
beyond this moment, the moment of his death.
THE KING. A week—nay, a day; see but a day;
see if I can hold them back but so many hours—
THE MAGICIAN. Do you think that your powers of war are to be the
only
sons of luck? is the haft of your kingdom more
than the craft of my mind? I see nothing; do you hear?
I who beheld—what did I then behold?
infinity? yes, except for one star
that was always moving there, and never where
my art expected. Here are your other friends—
back so soon? It seems something ends
their plenilunary content.

[The OLD WOMAN *returns; she is crying*

THE OLD WOMAN. Thieves! thieves!
My house was broken open and my floor dug up—
my money was gone: send, sir, some guard
to take the thieves. I am a poor woman
and had hoped to have peace in my last days.
Send someone to hunt the thieves, my king.
THE KING. You are not like to have peace, nor I neither.
Something more will be here soon to strike.

THE OLD WOMAN. What do I care if your enemies share your
    crown?

, I shall wait until they pass; the grass that grows
    in a palace gate finds soil too poor at a hut's.
    All that I need is freedom from my son's wife.

                                  [*The* LOVER *enters*

THE MAGICIAN. And your life, young man?

                      [*The* LOVER *looks at him terribly*
                                 It began well.

Who would have thought the death of a god could change
    what (it seemed) fell beyond the gods?

THE LOVER. Be still: he said right; this is a city of youth.

THE MAGICIAN. Love is kind to youth.

THE LOVER.   Love is . . . old man,
    take care; the heir of love is a torn heart.

THE GIRL. Were you happy?

THE LOVER. Happy? We were fortunate and therefore happy.
    But you knew better.

THE GIRL.   Are you sure of that?

THE KING. If indeed Good Fortune is now dead,
   our god, our only hope, behoves all
   to put away our loves, and what may fall
   take nobly, to make a nucleus of hearts
   resigned with one mind against Fate
   to share what we have, and in natural honour brave
   all else. Resign yourselves; be strong.

THE LOVER. Sir, that is nonsense; that is the talk
   of men who believed once that loss might occur.
   Never was I of those. Woes might be,
   but this is more than grief, and yet belief
   rages in me, delirious but unable to die.
   Good Fortune may be dead for you, but for me
   his spirit roars here, demanding godhead,
   nay, having it: I will not be resigned.

THE KING. What will you do then?

THE LOVER.   I do not know what I will do.
But I will not be content; it is all untrue,
this content, this resignation: love must live,
and if a woman coils up in another's heart
and spoils love's accidents, love's substance must gather head,
I do not see how, but somehow: love must live.

THE KING. That he could do while Good Fortune lived.
But I must lose my crown now, and why
should you show less content? all the earth
is resigned: why should a lover's mind escape?

THE LOVER. Because his love is more substantial than yours.

                                          [*To the* MAGICIAN
Master, though your knowledge fails, you are not unwise.
Which of us two is true?

THE MAGICIAN. Either; go you
living in death and he dying in life.
Toss for your choice.

THE KING.   Which did the stars say
was the wiser? which is the power in your own mind?

THE MAGICIAN. Give me your hands; there is much power in the
    hand.
My predecessors say that all enchantment
is summed in the free hand; therefore a priest
fetches blessing out of the air with his,
or a woman stretches hers to love and be loved
with the palm's inward: give them; if the gods die,
let us see, wherever rage and resignation endure,
what cure there may be.

                                          [*He takes their hands*
                      Now the shrouded battle
in my brain halts; I see the unclouded stars
sitting still, as if they were the will of Nature,
of substance the creature. I see, between two skies,

the great stars, the million hints of perfection,
stretching far away, and I see the moving star,
spending its glory everywhere, and not losing,
descending: is it devising to earth—and here?
It is coming down; the earth is drenched with it;
blenched on high, its great companions sit,
fit to be watchers of fate, but not fate;
fate is the stolen gold and the false love
and the lost battle, in the death of all good fortune.
Hold yourselves; veil yourselves; the core
of the moving star shoots at my back; who
waits in this city to be clothed with the star?

[*He whirls round on* MARY

Woman, by the star that glides into your frame,
by the path that Nature hides from all wizards,
by the wrath and the resignation of death, speak!

[MARY *remains silent*

Mother of the only moving star, speak!
Mother of disaster, mother of destiny, speak!
Mother, if you are a mother at all, speak!

[*He falls on his knees*

MARY. I will speak because you know of what I speak:
you, wizard, though you do not reach it, know.
But tell me first what you think you wish to know.

THE MAGICIAN. It can only be spoken under great veils,
since it is we who must be what we wish to know:
when all fails, what is the right thing to be? ✓

MARY. You must be as you can. I say only, when all fails,
then is the time, brother, to work a little. ✓

THE OLD WOMAN. No work will fetch me my warm room
where I can be alone or ask who I like.
I worked once; now I want to rest;
how can I rest in my son's wife's house?

MARY. My own Son sent me to live in another's.

38

I have no mother's word for any woman,
sister, beyond this terrible biting word.

THE KING. Tell us this difficult biting word.

MARY.   No;
biting but not difficult; quite simple.
When your god Good Fortune dies, the only thing
is to bid your god Good Fortune rise again.

THE OLD WOMAN. That is silly.

THE KING.   That is impossible.

THE LOVER.   That is true.

THE GIRL. O do not say so, do not say so; I know it is true.

THE MAGICIAN. Do it.

MARY.   It is a great risk you run.
You may not, when it is done, much believe it.

THE THREE MEN. If it can be done, we can believe it.

MARY.   Can you?
We shall see; I will do it anywhere for any who ask—
on seas or in cities; wherever Good Fortune dies,
there am I to bid him rise, if you will,
after his proper manner.

> [*She goes to the body and touches it; then she stretches her
> hand over it*]

Good Fortune, god Good Fortune, do you hear?

> [*She pauses*

Good Fortune, dead Good Fortune, do you hear?

GOOD FORTUNE [*in a dead voice*]. I hear; all the dead shake before
you.

MARY. Where are you?

GOOD FORTUNE.   In a dry place, between two skies.

MARY. Go forward. . . . Where are you?

GOOD FORTUNE. Among millions of stars;
it is difficult here even for the ghost of a god
to move forward, as my substance makes me move.

MARY. Sparks of perfection, shining hints of perfection;
  between the hints, sparks, and slivers of perfection,
  go forward. . . . Where are you?
GOOD FORTUNE.   Dying in death.
THE LOVER [*murmuring*]. That is it! that is it! that is where I am
  now.
MARY. Where are you?
GOOD FORTUNE.   Under a shape crucified and burning.
MARY. Go forward. . . . Where are you?
GOOD FORTUNE.   Your voice is behind and before me.
  I am before you; you are on a throne.
  A child is standing on your knee; a small hand
  blesses everything, though nothing but I am there.
  It is marked with a dark ring of dried blood.
MARY. What does he say?
GOOD FORTUNE.   He says: 'Live, Good Fortune'—
  woman, woman on earth, tell me to die.
MARY. What is he doing?
GOOD FORTUNE.   He has taken my heart from my side,
  and is twisting it in his hands.
MARY.   Untwisting.

                                       [*She pauses*

  Live; do not sleep; tell us what he says.
GOOD FORTUNE [*moaning*]. O. . . he says: 'Good Fortune, you have
    your fortune;
  yours is the only fortune; all luck is good.'
THE LOVER. That is it! that is it! all luck is good.
  Why did you tell me to be resigned? Fool!
  Why did no one tell me?—all luck is good.
THE GIRL. Dare you say it?
THE LOVER.   Dare you not believe it? up!
  bear up with me and say that luck is blessed.
THE MAGICIAN. This is the track of the single moving star,
  between motionless stars: all luck is blessed.

THE KING. How is it true there is no evil fortune?
  it is evil fortune to lose my crown and my head.

THE OLD WOMAN. To be bullied by my own son and nagged by his
    wife;
  it is silly to call that kind of luck good.

MARY. It is done; you must make your own choice now
  and show as you will. Live, Good Fortune, live.
  Live and return and tell us what you know.

GOOD FORTUNE. How shall I be able to tell you what I know?
  I found myself riding through the heavens; below,
  on earth, wise men were riding to a Birth,
  to a lonely, difficult, universal gospel
  of the nature, its nature and all things' nature.
  The star in which I stood was moving to a loving
  between the Mother and the Child, and as I saw
  I became other than I was and a new creature;
  I was the master of all chances; all chances
  made the multiple star in which I rode.
  Therefore it shone, and now I take a new name
  that came when the Child smiled for the sake of its Mother:
  I will be called Blessed Luck for ever;
  the temples fall; and all kinds of fate:
  blessed is the Nature and the Fortune in the minds of men.
  Who among you all has professed me now?
  who moves with me to welcome all chances that may come?

THE MAGICIAN. This I know, if I do not believe: here am I.

THE LOVER [to the GIRL]. Say.

THE GIRL.   Say for me.

THE LOVER.   I will say for both—
  this we believe, if we do not know: here are we.

THE OLD WOMAN [to the KING]. Will you agree?

THE KING. Why should I agree?
  I think it makes sense and I think it does not;

if I have found defeat is there no defence
less wild than this?

THE OLD WOMAN.   And how can I agree
when I think my child hates to have me there,
my own son, and I nowhere else to go?

[*She screams out*

You! Stop! what do you say it all means?
I only ask common honesty in the gods.
Do you say, you fellow who pretended to die,
that whatever happens to me is equal good fortune?

GOOD FORTUNE. Yes.

THE OLD WOMAN.   It means nothing to me.

THE KING.   Something
perhaps, but nothing I have any hope to be.

[*They turn to go*

MARY. Sister, only those whose hearts are broken
might at a pinch blame you, but not here.
Brother, if you will not push to the last inch
your knowledge of defeat, you must keep your heart unspoken.
But these here, they have to make the choice
or to know, at the very least, that the choice exists.
You have chosen your ways; be blessed; go with God.

[*To the others*]

And you, great ones, you must always make your choice,
or always, at least, know that the choice exists—
all luck is good—or not; even when the ninth
step is nine times as difficult as the first.

[*To the audience*]

And you—this has been sung a long time
among you, as among the cities your companions—
Antioch, Alexandria, Bologna, Paris, Oxford.
Substance moves in you; my lord your Son
loves you; choose your ways. Go with God.

[*They go out*

THE HOUSE
BY THE STABLE

A CHRISTMAS PLAY

CHARACTERS

MAN

PRIDE

HELL

GABRIEL

JOSEPH

MARY

*The Scene is in Man's house on the one side
and in its stable on the other*

THE HOUSE BY THE STABLE

Enter MAN *and* PRIDE

PRIDE. What, are you not tired? will you still walk?
  will you still talk of me and of us and of you?
MAN. I desire nothing better now, and nothing new.[1]
  It was a high and happy day when we met.
  Will you never forget it? and love me always?
PRIDE.   Yes:
  I will love you always.
MAN.   So I believe indeed,
  and feed on the thought—to be everlastingly loved.
  Tell me, how did this surprise come true?
PRIDE. It is no surprise—if you think what you are.
  Indeed, it were stranger if I adored you less.
  You are Man, the lord of this great house Earth,
  or (as its name is called in my country) Sin;
  you are its god and mine; since you first smiled
  and stretched your hand to me and brought me in,
  since our tenderness began, I have loved you, Man,
  and will—do not doubt; kiss me again.
MAN. You are my worshipful sweet Pride; will you be
  so arrogant always to others and humble to me?
  Will you always make me believe in myself? I am Man,
  but before you came, Pride, I was half-afraid
  that someone or something had been before me, and made
  me and my house, and could ruin or cast aside.
  But when I look in your dove's eyes, Pride,
  and see myself there, I know I am quite alone
  in my greatness, and all that I have is quite my own.
PRIDE. So this wonderful house where moon and sun

---

[1] These first three lines may be omitted when a curtain is available.

45

run with lights, and all kinds of creatures crawl
to be your servants, and your only business is to take
delight in your own might—it is yours and mine,
a shrine for your godhead, and for me because I am yours.

MAN. Thus endures my love for my own Pride.
To thrust you out were to doubt myself; that
is a bygone folly now—I will do so no more.

PRIDE. No; do not: be content to love me.
See, to teach you (let me pretend awhile
that I can add something to your style—I
who am also and only your creature) I have brought here
my brother, born of one nature with me, my twin,
or a moment younger: let me call him in,
and he shall tell you more of what I have planned.

[*Enter* HELL

MAN. Are you my Pride's brother? give me your hand.
We must be friends; tell me, what is your name?

HELL. I am called Hell.

MAN.   And where, Hell, do you live?

HELL. Why, as to that, it is not easy to give
a clear definition of the place; it is not far
as your journeys go, and no bar to finding,
but the minding of the way is best found by going,
and that (of all means) best at my sister's showing.

MAN. We will go there some time.

PRIDE.   O soon, sweet Man, soon—
for, I must tell you, I have begged of my brother a boon,
first because you are my sweetheart, and next
because the laws you have made everywhere mean
you should have all the best. This is a brave
house you live in—and let me call it Sin,
because my tongue trips if I name it Earth—
but my brother in his country has a house braver still
and has promised it to us, of his own kind will.

46

MAN. Aye, has he? that is noble, and yet he knows
   perhaps I would take it from him, would he not,
   and I saw it one day and chose to have it for mine.

PRIDE. O love, how I love to hear you talk so!
   but for my sake do not be harsh to my brother;
   for your Pride's sake, smile at her brother Hell,
   and treat him well.

MAN.   Why, that I will do.
   How now, Hell, shall I have a house from you?
   Tell me of it.

HELL.   It is strong and very old,
   but (by a burning I have made there) never cold,
   and dry—the only damp would be your tears
   if Man could ever weep. The air provokes
   hunger often—you are so sharp-set
   you could almost eat yourself. The view is wide—
   heavenly, as men say in your tongue, to the other side
   of the sky at least, so far it seems away,
   and whatever is there will never interfere;
   that is quite certain. Because my sister desires
   I will give you this house if you choose.

MAN.   And because my thews
   are strong enough to take it too perhaps?

HELL. That also, no doubt.

MAN.   Well, let that be.
   You are a good fellow, Hell; you shall live there
   whenever you like, even if you give it to me.
   The three of us could be royal in such a house.
   We will have a drink on it first.

                                 [*He goes to fetch wine*

HELL [*to* PRIDE]. Have you seen the jewel yet?

PRIDE [*to* HELL].   No chance;
   I think he has forgotten where it is himself.

HELL [*to* PRIDE]. What have you been doing all this while?

PRIDE [*to* HELL].   Hush!

　I have a trick now; play to my lead.

MAN [*pouring out the wine*]. This is good wine; I have had it in
　　store

　more than I could guess; it improves with every flask.

　None could ask better. I must have tended the vines

　when I was young; there are no vines now

　or few: I have sometimes thought—were it not for my smile

　over it—the land would be more sterile than it was.

　Here; drink. You must need that.

PRIDE [*to* MAN].   Sweet,

　for Pride's sake throw him something in return,

　some trifle; I would not have my lord

　seem under an obligation even to Hell

　my brother—though indeed I meant well enough

　in persuading him.

MAN.   You are always right; no kindness

　but I am always just to pay it back.

　Now, brother, you must take something—yes,

　no words; I say you must. What will you have?

　Pride, what shall I give him?

PRIDE.   If you would be

　kind, play a game of dice—the best of three:

　it would please him; he loves a gamble.

MAN.   Dice? good.

　What shall we play for?

PRIDE.   Something quite small,

　or even nothing at all; the game is the thing.

MAN. No; something I will chance in return for a house.

　What?

　　　　　　　　　　　　　　　　　　　[*He drinks*

PRIDE.   A handful of dust of your own—Earth;

　or—if you want, as becomes you, to risk more—

　say that old jewel your servant talks

48

often of—more often than becomes him.
Soul, he calls it, I think.

MAN.   Soul? yes;
   truly he does talk thus; but if
   ever such a thing was, it has been tossed
   one day away in a corner of the house and lost.
   Besides, I have heard him sing sometimes of a bird
   that sat in the leaves of paradise and sang,
   and in his song he calls that bird Soul.
   I do not know; my paradise is I,
   and any soul that sings in me I will try
   on the dice any time.

                                        [*He drinks*

                    Look at me, Pride; you will be
   always faithful, will you not?

PRIDE.   Always, by my will.

MAN. I would kill you else.

PRIDE.   I am not easy to kill
   by any who have loved me. Sweet, we forget my brother.
   Come, let us risk this lost jewel your soul
   on the dice, let Hell have his chance of finding.

                                        [*Enter* GABRIEL

GABRIEL. Sir, by permission; there are poor people outside
   seeking shelter.

PRIDE.   Insolence!

MAN.   Who?

GABRIEL.   One
   from these parts, a youngish working man,
   and has his heart's love with him, his wife,
   a fair-faced girl, and (I think) near her time.
   It is a harsh night; if I may suggest
   she needs immediate rest—a room, and a bed.

PRIDE. Man, this servant of yours clacks his tongue
   more freely than mine should do; must you keep

E   49

rooms where any riff-raff tramps may sleep—
and have supper too, I suppose? you, sir,
I am speaking to you.

GABRIEL.   And supper, madam, you suppose.

HELL. Hey, you, speak well to your lord's guest,
my sister, or. . . .

GABRIEL [angelically]. Or. . . ?

MAN.   Rest quiet, Hell:
I have had this fellow for servant a long time,
ever since before I came hither, wherever
I was before I came hither; he suits.
He is neat and quick and keeps out of the way,
and looks after my accounts—at least someone does,
and it isn't I; let him alone.

                                      [He drinks

GABRIEL. Will you choose, sir, to speak to them yourself?

MAN. Why . . . it were wrong to turn a mother away
and pity to turn a woman, on a hard night,
in a plight of that kind; but tramps in my rooms . . . yet
one should be tender when one is comfortable, sweet,
tender to the poor, yes?

PRIDE.   I confess, dear Man,
I cannot see why; one cannot do what one would—
no, not you even, my bountiful god—
and (as things go) they are only encouraged to expect
more than anyone can do. My darling, have a care.

MAN. Well, there is that . . .

GABRIEL.   I think, sir,
you should see them now.

MAN.   Do you? Well . . . well,
just for a moment then; let them come in.
You are always ready to beguile me. And as for you,
Hell and my sweet Pride, be merry the while.

                        [GABRIEL goes out. MAN drinks

HELL [*to* PRIDE]. Surely that is Gabriel, that old gossip of heaven?

PRIDE [*to* HELL]. He? I cannot tell; angels and I
   never met much, not for me to recognize.

HELL [*to* PRIDE]. Your dove's eyes are not so sharp as mine.
   I have peered more deeps than you; besides, sleep
   takes you sometimes; it never takes me,
   and after a while he who wakes for ever
   finds the tingling and aching make sight the sharper
   in the land where the heart-breaking troubles the light.
   I am sure it is Gabriel; wait; show no sign—
   only be ready to whisper Man a little
   and keep your eye on the door.

PRIDE [*to* HELL]. Why, what can he do?

HELL [*to* PRIDE]. I do not know; nothing, I hope; if Man
   chooses to play, it is his affair and mine.
   But keep close; we may win the jewel yet,
   and Man get clear with us to my nice house.

                                             [*He sniggers*

PRIDE. Come, if you will see them, let us drink first!

MAN. Gabriel might have brought me more wine first.
   The curst fellow! he must be taught his job,
   and not to rob me of time for wandering tramps.
   Well, I have promised this time. Here, now
   let us drink to our union—

HELL.   Eternal, eternal!

                         [GABRIEL *brings in* JOSEPH *and* MARY

GABRIEL. Here, sir, they are.

MAN.   What do you want?

JOSEPH. Sir, shelter for one night, by your permission.
   Our mule has gone lame; the dark overtook us
   and all but shook our hearts with perils of the road.
   My wife is in no condition to go on.
   To-morrow we will be gone.

MAN.   Poor wretch!
She needs a fetch of care.

PRIDE.   Beware, sweet.
It is easier to let them in than to get them out.
You are too kind. Besides, if you have a mind
to go on this journey with our brother Hell,
you do not want strangers to rack your house
when your back is turned: anyone as great as you
must be true to his glory.

MAN.   She is a poor lass.

PRIDE. That is why; if she were of our class—
not yours; you are non-pareil—but my brother's and mine . . .
but do as you think best!

MAN.   For a night's rest . . .

PRIDE. To have people like these in the house—imagine!
But you, I know, are their master—and mine.
I am only thinking of your glory.

MAN.   Well, yes;
I see that . . . Gabriel!

GABRIEL.   Sir!

MAN.   Think:
is there no shed near where these could be stored
for a night in reasonable comfort? I can't afford
to have them inside; my Pride will not stomach it,
and yet I am loth to push them both outside
till their plight is a little better.

GABRIEL.   The stable, sir:
it is empty since you chose to dispose of your stud.

MAN. Good: give them a shake-down of straw there:
[*Half-aside to* GABRIEL] and hark! if you care to hand them a
hunch of bread
I shall look the other way.

[*He drinks*

52

GABRIEL. Sir, it is God's bread.
  I will do as you say.

MAN. O God, God!
  Why must you always bring your fairy-tales in?
  Did God build this great house Sin?
  Did God send this pleasant leman Pride?
  What has God ever done for Man?

GABRIEL. He gave that jewel your soul.

MAN. O soul!
  This is your old clack, Gabriel. In the whole
  of my vast property I never found it anywhere—
  with flesh, fish, or fowl. It must needs be some old
  hidaway rubbish. And what is God doing,
  if God is, being bounteous to me?
  For anything I can see, I had neither God
  nor father on earth: I was always just Man
  since the world began. You tire me; go,
  get them away.

GABRIEL. Sir, just as you say.

JOSEPH. Sir, a blessing on you for this grace!
  Thank him, Mary.

MARY. Sir, God will bless you;
  nor will my Son, when he comes, forget
  what you gave nor with what spirit. If
  he can be ever of use to you, I vow
  now, in his name, he will be well content to be.

MAN. You are heartily welcome. Gabriel, have them away.
                    [GABRIEL *takes them across to the stable*
  There, they are gone: now we can drink again.
  Pour it out, Hell. Pride, give me your hand;
  am I not a grand fellow?

PRIDE. Sir, just as you say!
  Nay, I love you, dear Man, for being so fine,

53

so full of your own importance. Do you not find
me more to your mind than a girl like that?

> [*While they dally,* GABRIEL *covers the Nativity, and the*
> *three sing the Magnificat, which* PRIDE *interrupts at the*
> *following points*]

MARY. My soul doth magnify the Lord, and my spirit hath rejoiced in God my Saviour, for he hath regarded the low
estate of his handmaiden: for, behold, from henceforth all
generations shall call me blessed.

PRIDE. Henceforth, we shall be the only blessed ones on earth;
and no generations of anything except our joy.

MARY. For he that is mighty hath done to me great things; and
holy is his name. And his mercy is on them that fear him
from generation to generation. He hath showed strength
with his arm; . . .

PRIDE. Be my arm of strength, Man.

MARY. . . . he hath scattered the proud in the imagination of their
hearts.

PRIDE. Imagine me in your heart.

MARY. He hath put down the mighty from their seats, and exalted
them of low degree.

PRIDE. Be mighty on me; exalt me to your great degree.

MARY. He hath filled the hungry with good things; and the rich
he hath sent empty away.

PRIDE. O rich, rich!—bear off, my dear;
no, my brother is here. Tower—will you?—
over me in your power? O but fling him too
your glory's world's wealth! let all my house
go down before your head's crown of splendour.
Tender us all our desires out of your greatness:
to him his gambling moment, his catch of chance;
then snatch me to yourself for ever.
Then, at the gate of your house, when we go

I will kiss you so . . . do you know? wait, my sweet!
Hell, have you the dice?

MAN.   I have dice here.
I used them often enough when I played with my friends,
but since I met you I have forgotten my friends.
Love of you tends to that.

HELL.   Do we play for a stake?
I do not mind; the game is enough.

PRIDE.   Yes:
but a stake, all the same, makes the game more amusing.
And, brother, you forget—you play for that jewel
called soul.

MAN.   Why, it does not exist, or if,
you will never find it.

PRIDE.   It will do; it is in my mind
that to play for the chance to find it is well enough.
What do you say, Hell?

HELL.   Aye; if I have his will
to lay hold of it, if I can, by my own skill—
nothing unfair, no force; but if it is found,
I take it in free exchange for the house and ground.

MAN. You shall, brother, for your sister's sake and yours.

HELL. However precious?

MAN.   Though it were worth my all.

                                        [*He drinks*

I am no miser; I was always open-handed—
was I not, Pride my lass? give me a kiss
and I shall win the game and my soul as well.
Two out of three; throw.

                                        [*They play*

HELL.   Five.

MAN.   Six. Ha,
that is my gain. Kiss me again, Pride.

PRIDE [*to* HELL]. Quick now, while he is blind with me.

[*While they kiss* HELL *changes the dice*

MAN. Well tossed, Hell; you have a knack, but my luck
is in now, and I back my luck to win.

[*He drinks*

GABRIEL. Man, where are you?

MAN.   Who was that called?

PRIDE. No one.

HELL.   The wind.

MAN.   It was a voice of some kind.

[*He looks out*

The rain is over; the stars are out; one
over the stable is more sun than star.

PRIDE. How slow you are! Man, your Pride is waiting.

MAN [*he is now rather drunk*]. Waiting, is she? let her wait then.
Why, you hussy, you are a part of me.
I am not to be called in as if I were Gabriel
to be scolded at pleasure.

PRIDE.   No; it was but that leisure
of ours, in Hell's house, I was wanting . . . but so,
just as you say.

MAN.   Ha, yes: again.
To it again.

[*He throws*

           Five.

[HELL *throws*

HELL.   Six.

MAN. What tricks . . . ? let me see. Six: it is—you have won.

[*He roars with laughter*

Ho, this is a fine thing we have done—
drawn the game.

HELL.   No; one throw more.

MAN. More? how many times have we thrown?

HELL.   Twice.

Hurry!

MAN.   What, hurry? what do you mean?
you are as saucy as this quean herself.

HELL. Throw; I am impatient for you to go.

MAN. Do you hear that, Pride? he wants us to go.
He wants to hunt for my soul.

> [*He roars again with laughter*

PRIDE.   No.

I do not think he will long hunt for that.

MAN. Well, kiss me—a kiss hearty and strong,
better than before; give me the winning throw.

> [*She leans over and kisses him lazily*

JOSEPH. Man, Man, where are you?

MAN.   Aye! . . . here.

Who wants Man?

PRIDE *and* HELL.   No one; no one; throw.

MAN. Someone wanted; someone called; who?

PRIDE [*seizing his hand*]. Throw—with me, thus; and I with you.

MAN. Let me go. I am Man; I will not be forced.
I will have you horsed on your brother's back, my girl,
and take such a cudgel to you as will crack
some of those pretty bones.

PRIDE [*to* HELL].   Throw first,
and he afterwards; or at the very worst
we will persuade him he threw and lost the game.

HELL [*throwing*]. Six.

MARY.   Man, where are you?

MAN.   That was the girl;
that was the pretty wife—hey, now
I am coming, Man is coming.

PRIDE *and* HELL [*seizing him*].   No; throw.

MAN. What is this? what is happening? How
do I hear a voice I have not chosen to hear

57

outside my house? Who made my house?
There was no one, was there?

PRIDE.   No.

HELL.   No.

MAN.   Then how
do I hear the voice of something outside me?
Or is one of you playing a trick on me? Pride,
if I thought . . . I am caught . . . my mind is twined in a voice . . .
it isn't yours . . . whose is it? Ho, you,
Gabriel!

HELL.   No; leave Gabriel alone.

PRIDE. Sweet, sweet Man, leave Gabriel alone.

MAN. No; Gabriel is my fellow; he will help.
He was here before I came hither; he suits.
He will tell me the voices. Gabriel, Gabriel, I say!

GABRIEL [*coming across in his magnificence*]. Here!
Sir, God made me and bade me wait
on this moment in your life: what do you need?

MAN. You are a good fellow: come here: listen.
My brother Hell and my leman Pride mean
to have me finish . . . that was not it neither;
there was something else . . . the girl, Gabriel, the girl.
I heard her call out: where is she?
Is she in danger?

GABRIEL.   No; she is quite safe.
This is the game, sir, is it?
                        [*He picks up one of the dice and looks at it*

PRIDE [*to* HELL]. Fool, you have tried too many ways to get him.

HELL [*to* PRIDE]. Damn him, who would have thought grace was
so near
as to hear that small squeak of a drunken voice?

MAN [*sleepily*]. The game, yes—but I don't know where we were.
Throw for me . . . the girl is safe, is she?
and her baby . . . hadn't she got a baby?

GABRIEL. She has.

Now.

MAN. Yes . . . to be sure. . . . Pride . . . Pride,
where are you?

[*He dozes off*

PRIDE. Here, darling, here.

GABRIEL [*catching her by the hair and pulling her back*]. Peace:
let the poor fellow sleep a little; you
would never be caught by anything as natural as drink.

HELL. Let her go. What are you doing there with my dice?

GABRIEL [*tossing the dice in the air and catching it*]. Dice—ha! So:
that is better.

It seems now to have only one six:
and now we can play the last throw again.

HELL [*whining*]. I won't! I tell you I won't! I won't play.

PRIDE [*snarling*]. Don't you, Hell: the nasty-minded scut,
pretending we cheated.

[GABRIEL *takes each of them by an ear, and knocks their
heads lightly together*]

PRIDE. Oo! don't—you hurt!

[*She drops to the floor, moaning and rubbing her head*

GABRIEL. You wanted the game; you shall win or lose on the game
by the luck of the game, but all luck is good.

Toil and spoil as you will, still in the end
the flick of every chance must fall right.

Throw.

HELL. I don't . . .

GABRIEL [*terribly*]. Throw.

[HELL *throws*

Five.

[GABRIEL *throws*

Speak—

what is it?

HELL [*cowering*]. Six.

GABRIEL. You have had a long run,
  you and all your tricks, but to-morrow's sun
  rises on a world where untruth is always untrue.
  That is simple enough but too difficult for you.
  Get to your house and the burning you made—and not even
  that is your own; the fire is borrowed from heaven.

> [HELL *goes*

And as for you, sister, you poor cheap
cowardly shrew; you . . .

> [*With an awful angelic effort he restrains himself*

I will teach you one lesson; kneel up; say after me:

> [*She obeys. He puts on his glory*

Glory to God in the highest, and on earth peace:
goodwill to men.

> [PRIDE *repeats the words, snivelling*

And now go.

> [*She begins to get up*

No; on your knees: go.

> [*She shuffles away*

MAN [*waking*]. I dreamt my Pride had gone.

> [*He stares round*

Where is she? what has been happening? call her, you,
  Gabriel.
GABRIEL. Sir, soon, if you tell me to.
  They will wait, I know, by the gate you call Death,
  which is the usual way to Hell's house.
  You may catch them there or yourself call them back.
  But there is a thing to do before you go.
MAN. What? do you bully me? I want my Pride;
  I want to be a god; she made a vow
  never to leave me.
GABRIEL. Nor did she—to be just.
  It was I—for this single night—made her go.
MAN. You are above yourself.

GABRIEL. Above or beside—
  distinct enough at least to deal with Pride.
  There is a thing that you must see to-night
  of your own sight, without Pride's arms round you
  or Hell's hand in yours. This one hour
  out of all time is given you to see it yourself.
  To-morrow things may change. The woman you saved
  half by your will from a little chill in the night,
  and from blistered feet, has a word to say. Come.
MAN. It seems I made her a poor offer, yet
  she was better in the straw than in the street:
  do you not think so? You look grander than you used.
GABRIEL. Sir, it is only that you give me more attention.
  When Pride is about, no one can see straight.
  You shall see more than I. Come when I call.

                                  [*He goes to the stable*

JOSEPH. Blessed one, what is your will now?
MARY. Dearest lord, to show Man my child;
  lest in some testy humour the rumour should fade.
  If he sees, his heart may radically move to love,
  whatever he forgets, wherever he sets his eyes.
JOSEPH. He who with all this Earth offered us the straw?
MARY. Did we deserve, dearest, under the law,
  this birth that I kiss? Nothing at all is given
  till all is given, I know; that is heaven.
  But then also it is heaven to know that all
  is given at once in the smallest free gift—
  even sometimes when only half-given. O my Son
  reckons as no arithmetician has done;
  he checks his amounts by the least and the greatest at once.
  O my Own, there are no, no accounts like yours!
JOSEPH. Blessed is he in his sole free choice!
GABRIEL. Lady, Man is a little drunk, and a little
  sleepy, with a little hankering after hell,

but yet also he has a faint hurt
at having offered as he did; if it pleased you now
to expose the Holy Thing—

MARY.   O let him come!
let him come quickly!

GABRIEL.   Man! Man!

                                           [MAN *stumbles across*

MAN. It is almost too bright here to see. Where
is the lady? I did give her a hunch of bread
and a place to lie; she might else have been dead.

JOSEPH. Do not talk nonsense.

GABRIEL.   Do not talk at all.

MAN. No, but I am trying to understand: why
should I who had one house, and another beyond
promised, have been so fond as to offer straw
in a stable? and yet . . .

GABRIEL.   Do not trouble your brain;
gain is as difficult to understand as grace.

JOSEPH. Do not talk, I say, lest the Divine One sleep.

MARY. Nay, let him talk as he will; he is mine; come,
Man my friend; it is true that but for you
I might have come to an end—here, at least.

                                     [*She gives him her hand*

Look, my Son thanks you.

MAN.   Was he born here?

MARY. This very night, in your stable; therefore, dear Man,
you, if you choose, shall be his god-father.

MAN. What will you call him, lady?

MARY   Jesus, because
he shall presently save his people from their sins—
and Hell shall play no trick on them more.

MAN. I did not quite refuse you, did I? or did I?
I cannot tell; Hell has made me stupid.
Did I deny you all or did I not?

Look now, he must have something to please him.
The house is full of things, and none right.
Stop; I remember something out of sight,
out of thought, but always I have had round my neck.

[*He fumbles at his breast and pulls out a jewel*

There; it was once bright; it might serve.
I do not know what it is at all.
But if you should want a bed for the rest of the night,
there is my room the best.

GABRIEL.   But this is your soul
I have searched for all this time!

MARY [*laughing up at him*]. Great Hierarch, even
the angels desire to understand these things,
and a mortal hand does more than the Domination.
Leave Man and my Son and me our mystery;
let us think our own way and not yours.
Look, I will breathe on it—so, and see
how it dances, and how my Beloved's glances follow.
Take it again, Man, a little while;
we will go up to your room.

[GABRIEL *and* JOSEPH *help her to rise*

Now be the gloom
of earth split, and be this house blest
and no more professed by poor Pride to be Sin,
for the joys of love hereafter shall over-ride
boasting and bragging and the heavy lagging of Hell
after delight that outstrips him—step and sight.

[*She makes the sign of the Cross towards the house*

Take us, O exchange of hearts! this we know—
substance is love, love substance. Let us go.

[*They go out*

GRAB AND GRACE

OR

IT'S THE SECOND STEP

(Companion and sequel to
THE HOUSE BY THE STABLE)

CHARACTERS

PRIDE

HELL

GABRIEL

FAITH

MAN

GRACE

GRAB AND GRACE

The scene as before. Enter HELL *and* PRIDE, *bedraggled and tired;*
HELL *carrying a large bundle*

PRIDE. No rest? no comfortable house?
    These lands are as empty of homes as our bag of food—
    yet I should know this place!

HELL.   Why surely this—
    yes, look, in this crook of the hills,
    look, here is Man's house once more!
    After this hundred years we have been wandering
    through the malignant lands, to think we have come
    again to your old home. What think you, Pride?
    Might it not be possible to find a rest here?

PRIDE. Why, it would be worth while to try; I
    and you too were so beshouted and bevenomed
    by that slug-slimy Gabriel that we lost our heads
    and ran too soon. Man cannot have forgotten;
    few do; their faithfulness to me is astonishing.
    Shall we knock, do you think?

HELL.   Prink yourself first.

PRIDE. This accurst mud!

HELL.   That dress will not provoke him
    under your yoke again.

PRIDE.   Look and see
    if we have anything better in our odds and ends.
        [HELL *opens the bundle, and they poke about: fragments*
        fall out]

PRIDE. I cannot think why we carry all this.
    What is this red stuff?

HELL.   A little of Abel's blood.
    A drop of that in a drink gives a man heartburn.

PRIDE.   And this?

HELL. Take care; a bit of Adam's tooth
   that he broke on the first fruit out of Paradise.
   He has had neuralgia in his jaws ever since.

PRIDE. And this—thistledown?

HELL.   The kiss of Judas.

PRIDE.   Judas?

HELL. You were sick of malignant plague when it happened—
   but the child whom Man sheltered when we had gone
   grew, and grew spoiled, and Judas, one of his friends,
   encouraged Man to kill him in a sudden brawl.
   There is no time now to tell you all.

PRIDE.   All
   meaning that when Man had got rid of me
   things did not go so well as Gabriel thought?
   You fool, Hell, why did you not tell me
   all this sooner?

HELL.   I had forgotten; my fits
   make me dull. We are not what we were;
   neither you nor I have ever been the same
   since the great earthquake and the talking flame.

PRIDE.   Hell,
   did we not hear that Man had a changed heart?
   I am sure that some antipodean rumour
   reached us of his altered humour; that he likes now
   prayer and servile monochromatic designs.
   Draggled decency might better suit us?

HELL. I will say, looking at our bag, it would be easier.
   May not you be converted as well as he?
   Try that style: [*He grabbles about*] look, what of this?
                          [*He holds up a dirty rough cloak*
   How of this for a man's earthenware embrace
   and a chaste kiss? [*She puts it on*] Your very face looks holy.

PRIDE. What is it?

HELL.   Devil knows; the original figleaves, I should think.
You will need a belt. [*He holds one up*] Jezebel's?

PRIDE.   My dear, too bright.
What's that?

HELL.   The cord with which Judas hanged himself,
afterwards used to tie Peter to his cross.

PRIDE. That is the very thing; give it here.

[*She looks at herself*

I don't know who Peter was, but if
he was crucified, it is something anyone might be proud of.
Pride in a nutshell! [*She wriggles*] with the shell of the nut inside.
Hist, someone is coming!

HELL [*throwing the things in the bag*]. Is it Man?

PRIDE. No; it's a woman; what the devil—

HELL.   Chut!
There's Gabriel! Out of sight till we find out more!

[*They hide. Enter* FAITH, *meeting* GABRIEL. *She is dressed
as brightly and sophisticatedly as is possible*]

FAITH. Good-morning, Gabriel: where is my lord?

GABRIEL.   Madam,
he was in the stables just now, but I think he has gone
back with Grace to the house.

FAITH.   The stables?

GABRIEL.   Yes.
He has not been there much since the Holy One died,
but this morning something stirred.

FAITH.   A word in a song!
O to-day is such a morning as I love,
cloudy and cool; one feels rather than sees
the sun heavenly: he is distilled in the air,
and my heart filled with his future; in the dawn
I made a new song, and would fain sing it,
if Man my lord were free to hear.

GABRIEL. Madam,
could he do better than listen to Faith's songs?

FAITH. Well, to be frank, that depends; but thank you
for the kind thought. I will go and find him out.
O loveliness, to feel day in the dawn!

[*Exit*

PRIDE [*aside to* HELL]. And will you tell me who Faith is, and
what
Faith, in that dress, is doing in Man's house,
and I in this—shroud?

HELL [*aside*]. Not so loud; hush!

GABRIEL [*looking round*]. You need not trouble yourselves to hush;
your smell
would give you away; surely it is Hell and Pride?
The old obscene graveyard stink; I think
honest anger and brutal lust smell pure
beside you.

PRIDE. Stew-faced bully!

HELL. Sister, be at ease.
Once he had power even over us for an hour,
but not twice thus, not twice.
Abuse you he may; he cannot turn you away.
He must let Man choose now for himself.

PRIDE. Are you sure you are right?

HELL. Of course——

GABRIEL. Of course he is right.
I could be, were angels ever other than glad,
a little sad to see you with more tricks.
But now Man has friends if he will,
and if you can cheat him, why, you must.
I can do no more than tell him who you are.

PRIDE. I will tell him that myself.

GABRIEL. So do.
You seem perhaps more true than most

70

is older than you. Indeed, he does not look it,
but your travels in the malignant lands have aged you
more than our millenia.

GRACE.   A thousand years
being as a day. Poor Hell, time to you
is a sorry plod-plod; even Man knows better,
but Hell of all pedestrians is the most tired.
And why are you here, little brother?

HELL.   What is that to you?
May we not talk to Man without your leave?

GABRIEL. Unfortunately, yes.

GRACE.   And is she doing it now!

PRIDE. And tell me, dear Man, how you are faring in Religion.

MAN. Well, I am trying to lead the Christian life.
It is not easy, is it, Gabriel?

GABRIEL.   Sir,
I do not think you have found it too difficult.

PRIDE. To lead the Christian life is always difficult.
How we have to work! digging, building,
giving alms, prayer. Do you pray much?

MAN. A good deal. Gabriel, what do you mean?

GABRIEL. Sir, only that you have been constantly helped.
This boy Grace does most of the work.

MAN. I know Grace has been useful, but to say
he does most—I was up as early as he
and as bustling round my property.

PRIDE.   That I am sure.
I know how dextrous and diligent you always are.

MAN. I will give praise where praise is due, but something
is due to me.

PRIDE.   Much, indeed.

GABRIEL.   Sir——

GRACE. Chut, Gabriel; you will never defeat her so.
Do not argue; make her come out with herself

73

quickly; believe me, it is your only way.
Call Faith; she is better than you at the game,
and can frame a neater trap, woman to woman.

[GABRIEL *goes out*

PRIDE. It is no credit to any cause not to know
if one has kept its laws well. Flaws
will come, but when one has minded laws—why,
then a certain proper pride may grow.
I have taken Self-Respect for my new name
to adjust properly praise and blame, to keep
myself in mind as a true centre for myself.

MAN.   True.
One has more belief, so, in what one can do.

PRIDE. That is it: no weakness, no false meekness.
This humility is too much praised.
One may look at oneself, I hope, without sin.
You, my Man, can keep your thought so poised
that any noised silliness does not hurt.
You are pious—good! but it is *you* who are pious.

MAN. I had not thought of that. Faith sings
only about Immanuel and what he does.
That brings a sense of vacancy sometimes.

PRIDE. Yes: one needs at first a kind of defence
against even heaven. Perfection comes slowly;
and we must not be too holy all at once.

[*Enter* FAITH *and* GABRIEL

FAITH. Good-morning, my lord.

MAN.   Good-morning, Faith.

PRIDE [*to* MAN].   This
is another friend of yours?

MAN.   Her name is Faith.
She was a friend of Immanuel, the child born
the night you went. . . . O well, Pride—
I beg your pardon; it is old habit in me—

we need not go into all that now.
There was a misunderstanding of what he meant
and a tussle—you, my dear, will understand
there was something to be said on my side;
but anyhow—it was all rather unfortunate—he died.
But he left with me these two friends,
she and the boy Grace. Let me introduce——

PRIDE. She will despise me, Man. I am poor
and of no account, but I have enough respect
for myself not to push in among the elect,
among—look at her clothes!—my ostensible betters.

MAN. Clothes—nonsense. You look very nice—
quiet and . . . becoming.

PRIDE.   Man!

MAN.   Well, I
have you in my mind as you were when . . . but come;
it suits you. You are my own Self-Respect,
and this is my own Faith; you must know each other.

                             [GRACE *whistles*

Faith, this is an old friend of mine,
called—do I say Sister?

PRIDE.   Yes—I suppose,
Sister.

          [*She clings to his hand and looks deep into his eyes*

MAN. . . . called . . . Sister Self-Respect.
And this, dear friend, is Faith.

PRIDE.   Pleased to meet you.

FAITH [*coldly*]. Good-morning.

PRIDE.   Is it not a good morning?
[*To* MAN] This house was always good in the spring days.

FAITH. You have known Man a long while?

PRIDE.   Very long.
[*To* MAN] Of course, times change; I know now
you have other friends.

FAITH. Yes.

MAN. No.

You must not say so; at least, if I have,
I do not forget my old.

FAITH. It seems not;
especially when they return in a neat religious
habit, and are prettily disposed to public prayer.

PRIDE. What do you mean—public?

FAITH. I do not mean
praying with others present, but rather that sedate
praying to oneself, with oneself too as listener;
a ubiquitous trinity of devotion the temple-Pharisee
practised long and successfully.

PRIDE. At least I
earned my lodging here by a decent return—
by something other than songs; night was my time.

FAITH. Yes; *my* joys encourage sight,
accuracy, and reason.

PRIDE. My kisses were accurate:
Man enjoyed them and himself and me.
I did not confine myself to singing him songs.

MAN. O now, Self-Respect, they are beautiful songs.
Everyone to his own gift . . . indeed,
you always had beautiful shoulders.

PRIDE. Have I not?
as beautiful bare as hers bundled on Sundays?

[GRACE *whistles.* HELL *creeps towards him*
I am sorry, Man. I did not mean to snap.
I had better go.

MAN. O no, you must not go.
We shall all be great friends—I, Man,
and his Self-Respect and his Faith: why not?

FAITH. His Self-Respect and his Faith! No. Man,
you must make up your mind. There is a strong feud

76

renewed for centuries, from our very making, between
this lady and myself.

PRIDE.   There is indeed—
between my pleasure and your procrastination,
you promising what you do not pay,
and I paying what I need not bother to promise.

                        [GRACE *whistles*

HELL [*to* GRACE]. Stop that noise!

GRACE.   Noise yourself;
Adam called the birds on that note
while you were squeaking and squealing among the crocodiles.
O crocodiles' guiles and smiles and wiles,
when Hell styles himself a judge of music.

             [HELL *threatens him.* GRACE *trips him.*

Heels up, gossamer!

MAN.   Less noise over there!
Grace, keep yourself quiet in your own place.
Now, let us agree here to be friends.
Love puts all ends at one, and spends
much to do it: come, wine for a pledge.
Gabriel!

GABRIEL.   Sir, the ladies will never agree.
If you wish to turn Faith out of doors . . .

MAN. What! my friend's friend! Immanuel's friend . . .
why do you remind me? No; I promised; I am firm.

GABRIEL. Then send Pride away.

MAN.   O now, Gabriel,
I owe her, after all, a great deal,
and she understands me, she soothes me.

PRIDE.   I am not Pride.
Indeed, Gabriel, I have forgotten all that.
I am the old woman on the new way:
look at me, a demure modest Self-Respect;
nothing spectacular or dishonourable about *me*.

Of course, I am not *blind*; I cannot help
noticing where sinners thrive, or where they sin,
or how parasites and amateur prostitutes are dressed.
FAITH. The professional always hates being outclassed—
I agree there: for the word—let it stand.
Our feud, on my side, is too deep
to use abuse. I say I will not sit down
nor eat nor drink nor sleep in the same house
with—Self-Respect. I do not and will not know her.
PRIDE. And I—*I!*—used to be called Pride!
Is this your charity, you over-painted, over-powdered,
verminous haunch of a hag-bone! you snorting porcupine,
pet of a fellow whose hands never kept his head!
Why, you dilly-down doveling, you mincing mosquito——
      [GRACE *whistles.* HELL *runs at him; they dodge out, shouting,*
        while PRIDE *is screaming and* FAITH *speaking*]
FAITH. I will not abuse you. I simply will not know you.
MAN [*shouting*]. Silence! Gabriel, keep the house quiet!
See what Grace is doing and tell him not to.
And now, you two, am I to say nothing?
Am I not to have my own way?
You shall behave in this house, both of you,
as if I were someone.
PRIDE.　　　　　　O Man,
that is right! keep us in order; send us to prayer.
Rebuke us! Have I hurt you? O beat me
if I disturb you! I am only yours—
and of course God's; but I *am* wholly yours
in a new love, if you choose!
MAN.　　　　　　This fiddle-faddle!
Argument in, argument out. Man
will have his way sometimes; if I choose
you shall both stop with me, stop you shall.
I will tie you up, Pride!

78

PRIDE.   Anything, anything!

[GABRIEL *has been looking out*

GABRIEL. Sir, look!

MAN.   What is the matter now?
  What are they doing there? who is the fellow?
  Why, it is Hell! Was he here too?

GABRIEL. He is throttling Grace!

MAN.   He is throwing him into the lake—
  he will drown; it has no bottom. Hi!
  Hell there, Hell, leave him alone!
  Grace, we are coming!

[*He runs out*

GABRIEL.   Sir, Grace can swim;
  indeed, there is very little Grace cannot do—
  for example—get out of a bottomless pit.
  Well, it is proper that Man should run fast
  when heaven seems in danger; heaven has done
  as much for him.

[*He goes leisurely out*

FAITH. O sister, sister, now we may talk sense.
  You must find it exhausting always to be
  on guard, watching every word. Myself,
  help though I have and celestial succour,
  I am glad sometimes when my sister Hope
  takes my place for a night; and I can speak
  right and direct; the muscles in my face
  are controlled naturally and not by sheer work
  to please Man's variable moods. Poor Man,
  he is a sweet darling, but O I wish
  he had an adult intelligence.

·PRIDE.   You can drop this feud
  when Man is not here!

FAITH.   He is a born mimic,
  and therefore I must refuse to have you here,

79

or you would catch him with one or the other ruse.
Alone, we may leave it to God.

PRIDE.   Why are you so bent
to have him? he will never do *you* good.

FAITH. To obey Immanuel is in my blood; and he
chooses so. But how will Man serve *you*?

PRIDE. O yes; when we have him—as we shall;
you will call one day to an empty house;
anything else is not possible; well, then,
while your songs echo and re-echo, none
to mark them, except perhaps the sun in heaven,
think that Man is another vagrant I
and Hell shall sometimes meet where the sky
has no sun, in the clammy malignant lands
that Hell once made.

FAITH.   And now finds
everywhere terribly following him; even here.
O I know well wherever you go,
he and you, you sooner or later feel
the air of the cold iceberg or hot oasis
breaking into the same clamminess, the same
disgusting invisible froth against the skin—
ugh! every wind, every rain-drop,
every grateful beam crawling and sticky.

                 [HELL *creeps in behind her, making signs to* PRIDE

PRIDE [*getting nearer*]. Yes; we shall have a companion then, to bear
the bag over there of the odds and ends
we stole out of his house; in a dim mist
he shall stumble after us, afraid to lose even us,
or sometimes be pricked by me or kicked by Hell
forward before us, among the shallow pools
or the miry grass under the malignant trees
where the baboons sit and scratch and yowl.
There with us tramping and trapesing for ever.

FAITH. Poor wretch! but you haven't . . .

                [HELL *seizes her.* PRIDE *covers her mouth*

HELL. I have thrown Grace into the lake; quick.
  Shove this cloth in her mouth; tie it.
  If we can hide her we may lure Man
  out of his house into the malignant lands.
  Keep him till the sun sets and leave me alone
  to draw him down among the pits and pools.

PRIDE. Twist her arms behind her: use your fist.

          [HELL *strikes at* FAITH; *she dodges*; *he hits* PRIDE
  Damn! O anyhow: be quick.

HELL. Give me that cord; they will be a few minutes.
  Hang on to her wrists while I tie her legs.

PRIDE [*panting*]. She is so supple.

HELL.   All right. Now—
  in front then—pull! there. Where shall we put her?
  behind that tree?

PRIDE.   No; Hell, the bag!
  the bag! throw our things behind the tree,
  anyhow, in a heap, and then have her in.

HELL. Excellent! empty it. Now—over her head!

                [FAITH *digs him in the stomach*
  Ouch! Her hands are about as delicate as iron.
  There . . . steady . . . *there*. That settles Faith.

PRIDE. She can have her feud all to herself there,
  and fill her belly with her own gaudiness.

HELL.   Here—
  help tie it under her feet; so.
  I hear them; quick; carry it over here.

        [*They carry the bag to the back.* MAN, GABRIEL, *and* GRACE
          come in]

MAN. Hell, this is outrageous. He might have been drowned.
  O yes, I know he is a tiresome boy.

G   81

I am sure he provoked me often, his jokes
and his insolence, but to treat him so—
HELL. I would have seen to it he came to no hurt,
 had you not been by: since you were—
 But I was rash. I agree I did wrong.
 I apologize—gentleman to gentleman. As for him—
 here, lad, and another time watch your tongue.
 Catch!

           [*He throws him something*

GABRIEL.   One of the thirty pieces, was it?
 Grace will win them all back, one day,
 and not by playing dice.
MAN.   Well, now . . .
 where is Faith?
PRIDE.   Gone into the house.
 She would not even take the air with me;
 she preferred her own room to my company.
 [*aside to* HELL] For the devil's sake give me a better belt;
 I can't keep my things together.
HELL [*aside*].   Jezebel's?
 It is all we have.
PRIDE [*aside*].   Any damn thing.
 Your friends, dearest Man, are a little difficult.
 Faith is rude to me and Grace to my brother—
 not that I mind—and I (poor soul!) thought
 just for once I would replace the cord
 of my habit with a little brightness, my old lightness
 of heart took me so to be with you.

           [*She puts on the belt*

 Does it look silly?
MAN.   No, but more like you.
PRIDE. Of course, I do forgive your friend. You know
 that is where Religion helps. One can forgive.
 Is it not pleasant, dearest, to forgive others?

82

It is far sweeter than anger, more satisfying.
Lying in bed at night, I love to think
how many sinners poor little Self-Respect
has forgiven—even in a week or so. To be oneself
is always to find how much better than others
one surprisingly is. I take no credit,
of course, for that, though indeed, Man,
you loved me: did I seem—never mind.
You loved me.

MAN.   Yes.

PRIDE.   It was something of a joy.
Did you not feel yourself to be noble then?

MAN. Yes.

PRIDE.   O come for a little; come!
No, not in the house—out here,
away from all your people. Yes indeed,
I know we now are otherwise turned
and so will be; but an hour—come!
You shall be true to Faith and I to my vows;
only a little walk, a little murmur,
a reverie, a day-dream, a distant noon-glimpse
of our past joy, a thing forgotten but
for just this one companioned glance,
this twy-memoried gleam far below.
Come.

MAN.   I have never been able to forget you.

PRIDE.   Come.

MAN. O how the blood runs quicker! O—
Pride, Faith's songs are very sweet
but strange, alien with that accent, sweet
terribly, but to be with you is to lose terror,
to lose the beauty that strips me of comfort. Pride,
that is a dull dark dress you are wearing;
your belt shows it up; it is not like you.

PRIDE. We will see if we can find something brighter,
　　more to my lord's liking; we might. Come.

　　　　　[GRACE *has been poking up among* HELL's *properties. He*
　　　　　plays a tune]

　　Would you not like to see me? no, say,
　　there is no dress for Pride as beautiful as she,
　　as you used to. Only for a moment; only for joy
　　of the memory; then back to Immanuel and Faith.
　　Kiss me and say so. Kiss me.

MAN. Hark a minute. Who is that playing?
　　It is that strange distant song
　　which pricks a point of fire in each joint.
　　Grace, what have you there?

GRACE.　　　　　　　　　　This, my lord?
　　I found it hidden in a heap behind a tree.
　　It is one of the dulcimers Nebuchadnezzar's orchestra
　　played at the grand show of the Three-in-the-Fire,
　　who became, unexpectedly, Four.

MAN.　　　　　　　　　　How Four?
　　Is that the song's name?

GRACE.　　　　　　　O my lord,
　　the tale is old: it was one of Immanuel's doings.
　　Faith afterwards made a good song
　　on the dance of the Four-in-the-Fire. Hear me play,
　　and see if your heart does not move to the steps of the Fourth.
　　Sit, my lord; here is something to sit on.

　　　　　　　　　　[*He begins to roll the bag out*

PRIDE *and* HELL. Leave that alone!

PRIDE. Man, make your servants leave untouched
　　Our few poor belongings. It is my bag
　　and my brother's dulcimer.

GRACE.　　　　　　Nebuchadnezzar's dulcimer;
　　stolen like Abel's blood and Adam's tooth

and all the rest, from this very house.

I only recover it.

GABRIEL.   Indeed, sir, you have

a right to your own antiques—to give to Hell

if you wish, but even Hell must not steal.

Your museum was unique, but that bag holds much.

Roll it nearer, Grace.

HELL.   Leave it alone.

That dulcimer never came from the bag.

PRIDE. Yes; it is mine.

HELL.   Yes; but not from the bag.

That is full.

GABRIEL.   Ah but what fills it?

Tell me that, Hell. And look at it!

It is moving.

GRACE [*striking an attitude and sepulchrally*]. And where is Faith?

HELL.   How do I know?

PRIDE. Back in the house.

MAN.   Something is inside the bag.

PRIDE. Dear Man, only my own pet scorpions.

I cannot bear to leave them behind; one day

I will show them to you, but not just now.

MAN. Scorpions! no scorpion ever moved like that.

What have you got there?

GRACE.   Aha!

HELL.   Man,

We did not come here to be insulted.

                    [GRACE *whistles*

GABRIEL. The bag, sir, is trying to attract your attention.

I submit that the whole affair is so suspicious

you have a right to open it.

HELL.   No!

PRIDE.   No!

            [*The blade of a knife appears*

GRACE. Ladies and gentlemen, observe the scorpion's sting.
Little sister, your scorpions may stab you yet.

MAN. It is opening all of itself. Nothing like this
has ever happened in my house before.

GRACE.   My lord,
nothing like my lady Faith and I
ever happened in anyone's house before.
Adored be the Omnipotence for ever and ever!

> [FAITH'S *head appears through the cut*. GABRIEL *and* GRACE
> *run to help her out*]

GRACE. Faith in a bag is Faith at her best!

GABRIEL.   No;
even Faith must flag when she is stifled,
and Faith with vision is wiser than Faith without.

FAITH. Faith—and Faith may say so—is pretty well smothered.
O this old smell of Man's horrors
clings to the cloth, the beastly evidence
of things unhoped and undesired,
the present substance of things past and unseen.
Pah!   [*She stands up*

MAN. Faith, who has done this? I vow
I will now do justice. I keep promise—
I? no; I do not see my way
or what to say, but I swear the promise shall be kept
that I made Immanuel when he leapt into heaven—
mocking (O I know it! I know it!) my serious sin.
Tell me, who has done this?

PRIDE.   One
who will finish her work!

> [*She snatches a dagger from* HELL'S *belt and leaps at* FAITH

HELL.   Fool, leave it alone!
She is immortal like us! O imbecile!

> [FAITH *catches* PRIDE *and bends her back, twisting the hand
> holding the knife*]

86

MAN. Drop that!

> [*He makes a movement forward*

FAITH. Stop there, Man.
She has challenged me alone and I alone
will take the challenge. Since you will not choose
by honour or love, will you take the mere fact?
Will you believe in the power?

> [HELL *moves;* MAN *seizes him*

MAN. A little else!
There shall be none beside to interfere;
that at least I can do!

FAITH. Blessed Man,
I will swear at the Judgement that you helped me here.
So, Pride, so.

> [MAN *wrestles with* HELL

PRIDE. Ah, beast!
Help me, Hell!

HELL. Pride, help me!

GABRIEL. Grace,
would not your quick touch finish the trick?

GRACE. I have brought them to a clear field! now yield
the weaker! well I know who that will be.
O Man, well thrown! poor Hell!

> [MAN *throws* HELL *and puts his foot on him*

MAN. Well sung, Grace! had you not found
and struck the dulcimer, I should have fallen to folly
deeper and darker, and my Faith died.
O the sight of the knife cured all.
Does she need help?

GABRIEL. Probably not. I have known
Faith live and thrive in odd places
by her own mere valour. Look now.

> [*In the final stress* PRIDE *breaks down; the dagger is twisted
> from her, and she falls*]

87

GRACE. Well done, Faith! well done, Man! So.

[He picks up the dagger

I thought so; Cain's old obsidian knife!
What will you do with them now, my lord?

MAN. I?

What have I to do with giving sentence?

[He moves away. HELL *rises*

It seems to me that when I say *I*
or when I think myself someone I am always wrong.

GABRIEL. Sir, you have known that all the time
if you let yourself think.

GRACE. O chut, chut!

Gabriel, you archangels are so stern—
let our sweet lord make his own discoveries:
do not be so severe on his human reason
you with your communicated heavenly intuitions!

GABRIEL. I too have—never mind. You are right, Grace.
This is not the place or the time for rebuke.
Sir, it is true that for ever in this house
you hold the high, the low, and the middle justice
over all things; yet, as Hell said,
they are immortals; they cannot be put to death.
I do not advise perpetual prison here,
not trusting Pride—nor, sir, to be frank,
thinking you would have much chance against her.
We have seen——

GRACE. Gabriel! Come off your grand angelic
passion for instruction. This is Man's affair;
I would swear (if I could) he would do himself right,
and us.

GABRIEL. Very well. Sir, what will you do?

MAN. Do? it is they have done their last and worst.

*[*GRACE *whistles.* MAN *looks at him*

GRACE [*hastily*]. My lord, I am sorry; that was old habit.

When I am sceptical I always whistle,
and as for doing their *last*—forgive me; speak.

MAN. Let them go then to their own place.
Up and out!

[PRIDE *rises*; *she and* HELL *look at each other*; *she screams*

PRIDE.   O no, no!
Man, I will repent, I will do better,
I will be good one day—no, to-day.
Do not send me out to the malignant lands;
do not send me out with Hell! Save me!

GABRIEL. Sister, it was your choice.

PRIDE.   No, never;
not with him. O Man, Man——

GABRIEL. Man is not to be asked now; he judged.
The execution is remitted to us. We
are his household; we wear his livery; we do his will.
The Mercy of God takes Man at his word
and enforces it, by us who obey him on earth. Go.

PRIDE. Man, I loved you——

GABRIEL.   Loved! O little sister,
if anything was wanting, that has finished all.
Call Love in and Pride is lost.

HELL. Come, sister; the journey begins again.

PRIDE. No, no! [*She rushes from one to the other;* MAN *hides his
    face*] Save me! You have not gone,
you have not walked with him among the pools,
beyond the baboons and the crocodiles, beyond all
but the quicksands that never quite swallow us, under a moon
that never quite lights us, in the death that never quite dies,
and *he*——

GABRIEL.   Is this Pride?

PRIDE.   No, no.
No Pride! O if you had carried that bag—

89

the things we stole from you are beautiful beside
the things he can fill it with.

FAITH. But what does he *do*?

PRIDE. Denatures.

GABRIEL. Denatures!

FAITH. O horrible! O
God, pitiful God, have mercy on all!

[*There is a pause*

PRIDE. Yes. Hell. I am coming to you, Hell.

[*She stumbles towards him*

HELL [*softly*]. The bag, Pride; do not forget the bag.
It will be filled soon down there,
and now it is your turn to carry it—harlot!

PRIDE. Yes, Hell. [*She fetches it*] Here it is, Hell.

HELL. Come then. [*To the others*] We will be back presently.

[*They go out*

GABRIEL. So. That is done. Now——

FAITH and GRACE. Sh-h!

GRACE. Gabriel, there must be many things in the house
waiting for you. The silver needs polishing
perhaps; or the accounts—think of the accounts!

GABRIEL. Grace, if you were not a Divine gift——

GRACE. Yes, but I am——

GABRIEL. You are. If you were not——

GRACE. I know; I know; you said so. The silver, Gabriel,
the accounts! the dinner! We must dine, Gabriel!
While Man is on earth, he must dine;
and I do better myself on a certain nourishment.
Remember Cana of Galilee!

GABRIEL. Cana of Galilee!
Really . . .

[*He goes out*

FAITH. It is the second step that counts.
My lord, I can say nothing now to cheer

a broken heart; only that mine too
broke; we are not adult till then—O
we are not even young; the second step,
the perseverance into the province of death,
is a hard thing; then there is no return.
Most dear lord, if I could do you good,
I would; as it is——

MAN.   O Faith, Faith, I loved her.

FAITH. Yes.

MAN.   I loved her; God knows how I loved her.

FAITH. Therefore God shall make all things well—
O agony! O bounteous and fell judgement!— . . .
When you want me, if you want me, I will come
quicker than you can think. The Peace be with you,
and Love which is all substance in all things made.

[She goes out

MAN. A second step . . . a second step in love . . .
What, O almighty Christ, what of the third?

APPENDIX

SEED OF ADAM

Charles Williams's synopsis, written for the programme; and his notes for an address delivered after a performance at Colchester, October 1937

SYNOPSIS

THIS Nativity is not so much a presentation of the historic facts as of their spiritual value. The persons of the play, besides being dramatic characters, stand for some capacity or activity of man.

Adam, after leaving Paradise, is seeking the Way of Return. His many children, descendants who form all mankind, are tired of the search, and prefer the occupations offered by the Tsar of Caucasia and the Sultan of Bagdad: one calling them to outer things such as trade, exploration, &c.; the other to inner, such as art or philosophy. All these are temporary diversions, and Adam attempts to recall them to their proper business. He fails. In order to save his youngest daughter Mary from their persecution, he determines to marry her to her young lover Joseph. Mary is characterized by a love of people and things in themselves, and has gone beyond the tiresomeness of personal preference. The Archangel appears to her, and declares the Incarnation; she talks to Joseph of the nature of Love, and they go on their journey to Bethlehem.

The Chorus meanwhile exhibit their fear of the coming of some terror upon them out of the ends of time and space.

At this point Adam (or Man) returns in the shape of Augustus Caesar. He has conquered and quietened the world, and he takes a census of all mankind, dead or living, in order to discover, if he can, any knowledge of the Way of Return. The census is completed, but Adam-Augustus is the only known saviour. A voice

93

interrupts, and there appears the Third King. The Third King represents the experience of man when man thinks he has gone beyond all hope of restoration to joy, and is accompanied by a negress, who is, briefly, Hell. The two are come at last to destroy and consume all mankind; they come to Mary first. The play ends with the overthrow of the destructive cannibal nature of man at the moment of the Nativity, and with the adoration of the Omnipotence.

NOTES

ADAM and Dullards of darkness, light's lazybones . . . but this did not take me far.

The shepherds and the Wise men (kings)—the poor and others. The poem on the kings—the imaginations. Original idea of the poor [*i.e. for the Shepherds*]: and in a few fragments I toyed with this notion. But it did not produce anything very interesting; and anyhow it was not a true contrast, unless I made the kings the rich, i.e. the great capitalists, which I was very ill-disposed to do (i) because I did not wish to save the capitalists easily in view of Christ's remark about the rich—at the Crucifixion perhaps but not just at the Nativity, (ii) because then I lost my Imaginations, especially my myrrh and Third King. And then Miss Potter wanted a Chorus, and the Chorus and the Shepherds would have been too alike. So the Shepherds disappeared into the Chorus. Mr. Eliot has made choruses a little difficult. I know all about the Greeks, but they do not prevent one being told one is copying Mr. Eliot.

Well, I went on brooding, and the Kings increased. But there remained the awful difficulty of how to make the thing interesting. Which do you find most *interesting*—I don't say which do you think most important—the Nativity or the latest murder? Well, *if* you found the Nativity most interesting you would be reading theology. And do you? No. I am like you. And as I considered this my attention hung about the Third K. I had originally

94

intended each K. to have a female slave—partly to use up Miss Potter's females, partly to give opportunity for dress—or the opposite, partly to combine both sexes in each imagination. A K. with a dancing girl, a K. with a geometrician or a scribe, a K. with something more dangerous than himself—darker, a Negress. There was my first Negress.

Meanwhile I had, in my usual way, abolished Time and Space. I was prepared to bring in anyone. After all, the Nativity was a local event, besides being universal. Augustus and so on. How did we, if we did, bring in Augustus? How did we keep in Adam and keep out Aug.? Now remark this is a real technical difficulty. There are ways of doing it—one might make Adam unnoticeable, or one might . . . I don't know. But as I saw Adam he was important; I did not wish him to get to be the Chorus Leader; the Chorus were rapidly becoming imperialistic. And then one of those admirable clicks happened, and I said to anybody: 'Good God! Adam-Augustus, Augustus-Adam.' Admirable—*if* it could be done.

Well, then there was Joseph—and the Blessed Virgin. I was quite clear that the old man leading a devout girl on a donkey was not for this play. There are profound and awful possibilities in it, and one day I will do it. But there is something of it in the later plays of Shakespeare, and as a rule it is safer *not* to go trying to reap what He left. I will put S. into a novel when I want him but I will not chase after him. Besides, was there not a Mahommedan tradition that he was young? I hope there is; I thought there was —good: let us have a young Mahommedan Joseph, and let us (incidentally) make the second King a Sultan. The captain of horse I threw in as a picturesque extra, though it fitted so well with poetry that I have done it over again in my Taliessin poems.

And a just man? This theme is not much in. But it exemplifies [the] difference. The B.V.M. and her characteristics: love of God—before [the] coming of God (as such) to her: what state? Love. The romantic pressure of the individual.

PRINTED IN
GREAT BRITAIN
AT THE
UNIVERSITY PRESS
OXFORD
BY
CHARLES BATEY
PRINTER
TO THE
UNIVERSITY

sins to their nature—and so catch more.
Double temptation when a sin pretends to be truthful.
HELL. No, sir. We need not trouble you to announce us.
GABRIEL. No need; here is Man.

[MAN *enters with* GRACE

HELL. Now!
PRIDE. Get away!
Much better for me to be alone. Man!
MAN [*to* GRACE]. We will build then; I have decided that.
The cottages are clammy; we need several more
and more to the mind of those likely to live there.
First, we must find an architect.
GRACE. O sir,
I know a fine one, in design and execution
better than any; all the worlds praise
his work these many days.
MAN. Who then is he?
GRACE. He is called the Spirit; those who know his degree
add a worshipful title and say the Holy Spirit:
that as you choose.
MAN. The Holy Spirit? good.
We will ask him to come while I am in the mood,
which passes so quickly and then all is so dull.
GRACE. Sir, purposes last.
MAN. Yes, but heavily.
Madam?
PRIDE. Man!
MAN. Do I—ought I—to know. . . ? I have met few
of your veiled kind; yet——
PRIDE. Man!
MAN. By my soul, it is Pride.
PRIDE. Yes. [*A pause*] Do you grieve?
Would you have me leave, without a word changed?
I will, if you say go.

71

MAN.   No; stay.

Where have you been? I have not seen you since——

PRIDE. Since your servant told—yes; they *were* lies.

Though indeed I was foolish then, now more wise.

But to mistake folly for foul thought,

to drive me out while you slept! Have you sometimes kept

a thought of me?—no; that is folly again.

I am professed now to other vows,

as my dress shows. I have even changed my name

and am called Self-Respect.

MAN.   What, you are one

of Immanuel's people?

PRIDE [*drooping*].   He has a use for all.

                    [*She turns aside and gets near to* HELL; *then aside*

What was her name? quick, the great sinner,

the woman.

HELL.   Mary Magdalene.

PRIDE [*returning*].   Even Mary Magdalene—

and so for me, who did not (I may well say)

sin as much as she—and was she more beautiful?

Once, dear Man, you thought me well enough.

MAN. It is astonishing to see you; you have not changed.

The same lovely eyes under that hood.

It is good to see you once more, my own Pride;

no, I must call you my own Self-Respect.

It is what I will try to remember.

                [GRACE *whistles*. PRIDE *and* MAN *turn away*. GRACE *and*

                GABRIEL *speak to* HELL]

GRACE. And here is poor old Hell!

HELL.   Little tin trumpet,

how do you know me?

GABRIEL.   O we of heaven

know you all. This boy, whom we call Grace—

he is part of Faith's household, and she of Man's—

72